Technology Tools
for
Young Learners

Leni von Blanckensee

EYE ON EDUCATION

6 DEPOT WAY WEST, SUITE 106

LARCHMONT, NY 10538

(914) 833–0551

(914) 833–0761 fax

Library of Congress Cataloging-in-Publication Data

```
Von Blanckensee, Leni, 1945-
    Technology tools for young learners / Leni von Blanckensee.
       p.    cm.
    Includes bibliographical references.
    ISBN 1-883001-73-0
    1. Education, Primary--Computer-assisted instruction.  2. Internet
(Computer program) in education.  3. Educational technology.
I. Title.
LB1028.5.V66   1999
372.133'4--dc21                                              99-10335
                                                                CIP
```

10 9 8 7 6 5 4 3

To Deevy, who at ninety, truly exemplifies
what it means to be a lifelong learner.

Acknowledgments

This book represents the combined thinking of many people who generously shared their time, ideas, and knowledge. I would like to thank Millie Almy, Jane Baldi, Burke Cochran, Joyce Hakansson, Cathaleen Hampton, Linda Koistinen, Patricia Nourot, Barbara Scales, and Judith Van Hoorn, all of whom participated in extensive interviews that broadened my understanding.

I would also like to thank the many classroom teachers who invited me into their classrooms, shared their ideas, and were willing to try out some of mine. Among these were the teachers at the three Pacific Bell Education First elementary school demonstration sites: Juarez-Lincoln Accelerated School in San Diego, Mendocino Grammar School, and Bryant Elementary School in San Francisco. In particular, Nancy Camp, Peg Palm, Sharon Quinn, Bob Birdsell, and Kristina Shoopack at Juarez Lincoln; and Jessica Morton and Deena Zarlin at Mendocino Grammar School, provided some of the instructional units and ideas described in the book. Many other examples came from teachers who preferred not to be named. I thank them sincerely and will respect that wish.

My gratitude also goes to Susan Silverman for allowing me to reprint her Pumpkin Patch Project, and to Brian Maguire, Susy Calvert, and the Maxwell Hill Gifted Center for allowing me to use the Monster Project. Three California schools graciously provided the photos for this manuscript: Paden School in Alameda, Juarez-Lincoln Accelerated School in San Diego, and James Randol Elementary School in San Jose. I especially appreciate the efforts of staff members to track down parental permission to print the photos. Thanks also go to two of my colleagues, Marcy Lauck and George Bonilla, who assisted in obtaining the photos and permission.

I received invaluable feedback from mentors and colleagues who were willing to give their time to read the manuscript draft. I thank you all: Jane Baldi, Gene Michaels, Jodi Reed, Nancy Todd, Judith Van Hoorn, Mary Tribbey, Fran Rebello, and, of course, Vickie Bernhardt, Director Extraordinaire of Education for the Future Initiative. Actually, Vickie Bernhardt had a much greater role in this book through a combination of encouragement, gentle prodding, and announcing to our corporate sponsors, "Leni is writing a very significant book!" Belatedly, I thank her for that act of faith. The Pacific Bell Foundation, Pacific Bell, and the SBC Foundation also deserve my gratitude; I especially appreciate the encouragement of Mary Leslie throughout this project.

Many others helped me to prepare the manuscript. Thanks go to Lynn Varicelli for her help with the graphics; to my husband, Hans von Blanckensee, for his help in editing; and to Linda Oronas, who proofread and formatted the text. Finally, I am thankful for the support of my entire family throughout the process, for their patience, and for their recognition that I was spending time on an important endeavor that I might otherwise have spent with them.

About the Author

Leni von Blanckensee has been an *Education for the Future* associate since 1993. She currently collaborates with school and school district leaders throughout Northern California to support their overall reform efforts, using school portfolios based on data for continuous improvement. She has also assisted the Pacific Bell Education First Demonstration Sites in integrating telecommunications technology across the curriculum and throughout their organizations. Her current work is supported by *Education for the Future* partnerships with the Northern California Comprehensive Assistance Center at WestEd (funded by the US Department of Education), the Pacific Bell Foundation, and the SBC Foundation.

Before joining *Education for the Future*, Ms. von Blanckensee was a classroom teacher for 22 years. She taught kindergarten for more than 10 years, and has taught children of all ages, including a special program for teenage mothers and their infants. Early in her career, she began to read child development literature and connect its principles to her own instructional practices. When Apple Computer gave a computer to every California school in the early 1980s, she received it by default—no one else wanted it—and so began her interest in integrating technology into the curriculum. At the school level, she was an instructional leader who was involved with program development, review, and improvement. As the president of the local teachers association, she worked collaboratively with the district to involve all staff in districtwide reform efforts.

Ms. von Blanckensee is a graduate of the Cornell University School of Industrial and Labor Relations, and has a master's degree in Educational Technology from San Francisco State University.

Table of Contents

Foreword

During the many years that I have been teaching educational psychology and child development classes to teachers, I have seen important ideas in education come and go because teachers lacked the necessary support to implement them well. Right now, educators and the media are focusing attention on "integrating technology into the curriculum" and "using technology as a tool for learning." It is far easier to tell teachers why they should integrate technology than it is to help teachers do it. Most difficult of all is to provide concrete examples that teachers can implement, to provide enough models so that teachers can then create activities, and to keep the discussion grounded in child development theory at the same time.

Leni von Blanckensee has done a remarkable job in doing all three. *Technology Tools for Young Learners* is an excellent and straightforward "how to" book about using technology in kindergarten through third grade, which teachers in upper elementary grades could easily adapt to their needs as well. The book includes numerous specific examples of learning activities and instructional units that are appropriate for young children. The first and last chapters provide the theoretical framework to which the author connects the many suggested uses of technology. The reader comes away understanding how these activities can be tied to state and local standards, to authentic assessment practices, and to other "best practices" such as cooperative learning or teaching through multiple intelligences. Throughout the book, stories about actual classroom experiences with technology help the reader construct the understanding that is necessary to move from reading about technology tools to implementing model activities and, ultimately, to creating new ones.

This is a highly useful curriculum book that shows how to use a hands-on approach to learning, supported by technology tools. The author demonstrates clearly that what we think of as adult tools—digital graphics, word processing, Web publishing, e-mail, and videoconferencing—can also be effective tools for young children as they work on open-ended projects. However, this is not a technology book in the usual sense; teachers will not learn how to operate their e-mail or how to create their own Web site by reading this book, although the author does provide some pointers about where to get technical help. Instead, this book does what previous books I have seen have failed to do; that is, to keep the focus on the curriculum while showing how to integrate technology.

What is special about this book is that it reflects the obvious classroom experience of the author, who spent 15 years as an early childhood teacher. Her own stories, and those of the many people she interviewed, give the book a richness that makes it a pleasure to read.

Judith Van Hoorn, Ph.D.
Professor, Benerd School of Education
University of the Pacific
Stockton, California

Preface

Although I was a kindergarten teacher for 10 of my 22 years in the classroom, and I have spent the last 5 years assisting schools and districts in their overall school reform efforts, I never imagined in my wildest dreams that I would be writing a book about young children and technology. In fact, the research and observations behind the writing of this book came out of empathy for K–3 teachers who did not feel that they had enough understanding of how to integrate technology into the early childhood curriculum in ways that were consistent with young children's development. By a series of fateful events, it became my job to help them do exactly that, and I found myself on as steep a learning curve as any of the teachers I was there to support. The questions that arose ultimately led me back to school in an educational technologies program and to the writing of this book.

In 1993, I became an associate on the staff of Education for the Future Initiative, a nonprofit organization led by Victoria Bernhardt at California State University, Chico, that supports systemic change in schools. Because the Pacific Bell Foundation (since merged with the SBC Foundation) was a primary sponsor, it was not surprising that we were asked to support the Pacific Bell Education First Demonstration Sites as they began integrating the Internet and videoconferencing into their curriculum. Each of the K–12 sites—three elementary schools, three middle schools, and four high schools —made a commitment to use the Internet, e-mail, and videoconferencing to bring the world into the classroom, in the belief that these telecommunication technologies could improve student learning.

Each school received ISDN lines (high bandwidth telephone lines for Internet connection and teleconferencing), routers to make the lines usable with the school network, and two videoconferencing units. The schools were expected to provide the network and computers that would make the Internet available to all students. Once the technology was in place and the teachers had been trained to use the equipment, it became clear that many of the schools needed assistance in thinking through how to integrate technology throughout the curriculum and the school organization, and in measuring their progress. I was fortunate to be part of the team that began to assist the schools in March, 1995.

In many of the schools, discussions that began with technology integration led to an examination of the very core of the school's vision—the school community's hopes, dreams, and expectations for its children. It was at these sites that technology integration was most meaningful. I was very comfortable working with schools in this "big picture" arena as it had been the focus of my work for several years. Once the schools became clear about their vision for increasing student achievement, and identified the instructional strategies that would support their vision, it became easier to create models for integrating technology. As upper elementary, middle school, and high school teachers saw what students could do through collaborating on the World Wide Web, by e-mail, and through videoconferencing, many became genuinely excited and quite willing to put in the effort to integrate the technology into their programs.

The following describes some of the upper-grade projects:

◆ Fifth graders corresponded by e-mail with marine biologists at the Monterey Bay Aquarium, as part of their research about marine animals. At the end of the unit, they took a "virtual field trip" by videoconference to the Aquarium.

◆ Eighth graders researched the Iditarod dog-sled race, in conjunction with reading *The Call of the Wild*, one of the core literature readings for that grade level. Their research and associated activities included corresponding by e-mail with "mushers" (dog-sled racers), tracking the race on the Internet, and interviewing a musher who visited the school with his dog-team.

◆ Eleventh graders at two high schools in different parts of California explored the meaning of democracy by sharing data via the Internet, that students had gathered from interviews. Students in both schools:

  • Interviewed adult friends and relatives about the meaning of democracy

  • Entered their data in a shared database on the Web

  • Analyzed the data

  • Read a collection of primary source material posted on the Web

  • Discussed the meaning of democracy via videoconference with Alexis de Toqueville as played by a history professor

  • Wrote papers about their research

The journey to integrate technology was much more difficult for the primary teachers (K–3). In the beginning, only a few became genuinely involved. Some of their colleagues expressed concerns about whether using telecommunications technology was developmentally appropriate for young children. Others were open, but could find few high quality instructional activities intended for young children. Generally, the technology coordinators who were available to help were more experienced with older students and had difficulty offering the needed support. Given the limited resources that were available, and the disparity of thinking among teachers at the K–3 grade level, it was clear that more information was needed, based on research.

I began a preliminary search of the literature with the intent of providing existing resources to the teachers at the demonstration sites. To my surprise, the existing literature dealt mostly with educational game software designed for young children, and very little with technology tools that are used for productivity in the way adults use technology. While one might guess that research on children's software would provide insight into using technology tools, there is not a direct correspondence. To further complicate the scarcity of information, the research was reported almost exclusively in early childhood education journals rather than in journals targeted to elementary schools, or educational technology journals.

Once I determined that current research would not provide the answers, I began to look to other sources. I chose a combination of interviews, observations, and informal discussion with teachers. I found nine experts in the field of child development and/or use of technology with young children who consented to lengthy interviews. Information about the interview participants, who provided many of the ideas in this book, is found in Appendix A. References to the interviews are included throughout the book because I believe that those who shared their ideas so generously should be specially acknowledged. In addition to the interviews, I observed children using technology and had many discussions with teachers in the course of my work with schools over four years.

Based on my own and many others' questions, I wanted to know what value young children would obtain by using technology as tools in their learning, and what would be the best uses. My investigation targeted the communication tools that were available in the Education First Demonstration Sites, and were becoming increasingly available at other schools:

- ◆ Graphic (digital) images
- ◆ Word processing
- ◆ Multimedia
- ◆ E-mail
- ◆ The Internet
- ◆ Videoconferencing

This book explores the many ways in which these "technology tools" can be used by young children, in much the same way that adults use technology in the course of their work. Information from the interviews, observations, and discussions are synthesized throughout the book, and references to other research are cited where it is useful.

Chapter 1: Beyond Educational Software describes the approach of the book, summarizes research that addresses concerns about using technology with young children, and includes the National Association for the Education of Young Children (NAEYC) guidelines on using technology.

Chapter 2: Graphic Images explores the use of digital photography by young children as a way to document and record their work and as a trigger for language development and writing. It includes discussions of clip art and of scanned original artwork used by children in their work.

Chapter 3: Word Processing and Literacy discusses the research regarding the use of this tool in the classroom, including "talking" word processors (text-to-speech). Keyboarding issues are also addressed.

Chapter 4: Multimedia Presentations examines how young children can design and execute components of multimedia, and the degree to which they can put the pieces together. It describes appropriate support from adults and older children that is needed for young children to use this valuable tool.

Chapter 5: The Internet describes Internet analogies, use of the Internet for publishing student work, and using the Web as a resource for information.

Chapter 6: E-mail shows how e-mail can be used to motivate children, to support their developing literacy skills, to encourage inquiry, and to promote multi-cultural awareness.

Chapter 7: Videoconferencing discusses uses in early childhood classes to develop ongoing relationships between classes, to supplement e-mail, and for special events such as virtual field trips.

Chapter 8: Getting Started and Finding Help describes processes for managing technology in the classroom, and describes Web resources and other sources of help available to teachers.

Chapter 9: Taking a Schoolwide Approach discusses the relationship between technology and school reform, points out the importance of coming to school-wide understandings about a vision for teaching and learning, and describes some of the factors that help schools become successful in integrating technology consistently with their visions.

Chapter 10: Child Development Theory and Educational Practice provides a resource for readers who want a review of child development theory, particularly that of Piaget and Vygotsky, and summarizes the concepts that form the base for Developmentally Appropriate Practices (Bredekamp 1987; Bredekamp and Copple 1997).

Examples of exemplary K–3 activities and projects using technology tools are found throughout the chapters. Many are easily adapted for upper elementary grades. In addition, Chapters 4, 5, and 7 each include a complete instructional unit appropriate to young children.

1

Beyond Educational Software: A Theoretical Framework for Using Technology Tools

Teachers who use computers stand at a crossroads facing three roads. Those traveling on the first road use simple computer games for rewards or occasionally use drill software; they do not integrate computer work into their educational program. Those traveling on the second road integrate drill and other structured software activities into their programs. And those traveling on the third road use problem-solving software and tools such as word processors, LOGO, and drawing programs to enrich children's education.

Research suggests that the first road is a meandering and useless one....The second road leads somewhere educationally—integrated computer activities can increase achievement ....This is a safe and easy path....The third road takes more effort, time, commitment, and vision, but it offers the hope of educational innovation.

Douglas Clements, 1994

Since 1994 when Douglas Clements wrote the words above, the number of technology tools that can support young children in their learning have increased, but the concept put forth by Clements still holds. In some classrooms today, children are documenting their work using computers in conjunction with cameras, video and audio recordings, multimedia software, and word processing software. They are communicating their ideas and collaborating with others through e-mail, Web publishing, and videoconferencing. Young children can use these technology tools in much the same way that adults use them. Technology can help all of us explore ideas, formulate them more clearly, and communicate them to others.

Imagine this:

As part of the social studies curriculum at your grade level, students explore community connections: the relationships between individuals, families, and people at work. Several state standards in social studies tie to this unit, and you routinely use the direct experience in social studies and science as a basis for classroom learning. You begin by having students share what they know and what they want to know, so that you can tailor the unit more closely to their needs and interests. From there, you plan a series of real experiences—children will see the work behind the scenes at the fire station, the library, the grocery store, and a local fast food restaurant.

This year, you take a digital camera and a video camera with you on the walking trip and record as much as you can. Children use the pictures to recall events, retell them in sequence, and help them formulate questions about what they have seen. Some of these questions can be answered in class; children use e-mail to get answers to the questions they cannot answer, and are delighted by the quick replies. As in the past, you ask students to draw pictures and write about what they learned. This time, they scan their pictures and use a word processor to add the text. You notice that the children write with greater depth and take their work more seriously when they have photos and videos to prompt their memories and use a word processor to record their thoughts.

You now have a collection of writing, artwork, photos, and video clips. Together the class plans a multimedia presentation that includes some of the photos and video and each child's writing and artwork. The children are able to construct their parts of the presentation with the help of fifth-grade technology mentors and you create the menu that pulls the work together.

All the children are excited about the magnitude of what they have done and want to share the project with their parents at the school's open house. Parents are equally impressed; afterward, one parent who has a local business offers to host your multimedia project on her Web site. As you discuss the open house in class the next day, one child announces, "Our class has lots of community helpers." These words hit home—in the process of using technology tools that help children to create their best work, you have discovered the potential of technology to build community as well.

Perhaps this story seems beyond the realm of the possible, yet the technology tools described in this scenario—computers, software, Internet access, cameras, and a scanner—are currently available in most schools today. This book addresses how to integrate technology tools so that they support children's development and learning.

Using Technology as a Tool

In primary grade classrooms, computers have been used mostly for educational games, often used as a reward or after the children have finished their other work. Educational games vary from open-ended to strictly drill-and-practice. Some are highly interactive while others barely interact with the user.

Even high-quality open-ended children's software tends to be used in parallel with instruction designed by the teacher rather than as an integral part of it. Teachers often use the software to reinforce skills and concepts that are taught in other ways. There is an underlying assumption in many classrooms that children will use these educational games independently, thus freeing the teacher to work with other groups of children. There is no doubt that high-quality interactive educational games can be quite valuable when used in conjunction with direct experience, yet educational games fall short of what the technology can potentially offer when it is truly integrated into the curriculum.

In contrast to what they are able to accomplish with educational games, students can use technology-based tools to create original work that is an integral part of the teaching and learning process. Technology tools are most valuable when teachers design projects that encourage children to push the limits of their current knowledge. The teacher acts as a facilitator to students, who construct ideas and develop skills as they work on real-world tasks. These *constructivist* instructional practices are intended to engage students of varying academic skill by connecting to and building upon the interests and existing knowledge of each student. The teacher provides guidance and support, but allows students to have a high level of control over their projects.

When technology tools are used in this way, the focus is on the students' work. The technology provides the support that encourages students to push their limits by thinking about and presenting ideas in ways they might not otherwise have been able to do. Cathaleen Hampton, technology coordinator at Alvarado Elementary School in Union City, California, has observed that using technology in this way requires a major shift of thinking on the part of teachers. Teachers must model the use of the technology, and support children's use until they can take over on their own (1998). As children become familiar with technology tools, they simply become part of the background as children work, yet what they add to the quality of that work can be striking.

**Figure 1.1. The Author's E-mail Buddies
Respond to a Message**

Some examples of technology used as tools include:

- Word processing for writing
- Digital cameras for taking pictures
- Scanners for digitizing artwork and photographs
- Multimedia software for making presentations
- E-mail for writing and receiving communications
- The Internet for publishing student work
- The Internet for finding information
- The Internet for sharing scientific data among classes
- Spreadsheet programs for organizing and displaying data
- Spreadsheet programs for graphing
- Databases for storing, sorting, and retrieving data
- CAD programs for architectural drawing

Notice that when technology is used as a tool, it is used *for a specific purpose.*

Not all of the listed uses of technology are appropriate to young children. At the upper elementary, middle, and high school levels, many books, journal articles, and Internet resources are available to help teachers integrate technology in ways that support constructivist, student-centered classrooms. Very little is available to help primary grade teachers integrate technology tools in ways that support young children's learning.

Viewing Technology Integration Through a Developmental Lens

Many K–3 teachers are aware that constructivist instructional practices, such as those mentioned above, are only one component of a program that serves the needs of young learners. It is also crucial that teachers incorporate an understanding of developmental stages and knowledge of each child's development into program planning.

This idea is based on the work of many child development researchers and theorists who believe that children progress through specific stages of cognitive growth, and that these stages are distinct and qualitatively different from each other. Stages of development are not defined by age—there is always a wide variation in developmental level among children who are the same age—yet they are age related. When teachers are knowledgeable about child development as well as constructivist instructional strategies, they are likely to provide a more appropriate learning environment.

This book is intended to support those teachers who already have a developmental approach and want more information about using technology tools to complement that approach, and to encourage others to implement technology in ways that are developmentally appropriate. Throughout the book, discussions of best practices will be related to current understanding of how children learn and develop. A brief summary of child development theory as it applies to the classroom is provided in Chapter 10.

Using a Child Development Approach in a World of Standards

Because of the current move toward standards, some primary grade teachers and administrators have come to believe that they must give up developmentally appropriate practices (DAP). As I visit schools, I hear talk of going back to workbooks and of using technology for drill as ways to meet the standards. This discussion stems from a misunderstanding of the relationship between DAP and standards-based curricula. Neither DAP nor standards are a specific program, nor are they necessarily in conflict with each other. Developmentally appropriate practices are the *how* of early childhood education—the creation of a learning environment that "takes into account everything we know about how children develop and learn" (Kostelnik 1993). Standards are the *what* of K–12 instruction—what we want children to know and be able to do. If the standards are high, as they should be, teachers have all the more reason to design a program in keeping with how children learn. It is through developmentally appropriate practices that children can best master high standards.

A conflict only exists when specific standards are inappropriate to young children (for example, expecting knowledge of astronomy before children can conceptualize time and space of such large magnitude). When this kind of conflict exists, teachers and administrators need to address the specific standard in question, armed with a knowledge of child development. We would be doing a great disservice to children were we to turn away from developmentally appropriate practices, including the appropriate use of technology, just because certain standards may not be appropriate.

Historical Concerns About Technology and Young Children

In the 1980s, as computer use in schools was growing, many questioned whether computers fit with early childhood education practices (Barnes and Hill 1983; Cuffaro 1984). Researchers began to observe and interview children who were using various types of computer hardware and software; in the decade that followed, these concerns were for the most part answered. Still, some primary teachers continue to voice the same concerns. The research cited below may be useful to those who continue to hear developmental arguments used against integrating technology in primary classrooms.

> *Computers are too abstract. Young children should be manipulating real objects in more physically active ways than computer use allows.*

Child development researchers have explored in depth the connection between using hands-on activities and using technology to assist in conceptual development. Most recommend that young children use computers to complement hands-on activities, not to replace them.

Piaget provides us with the understanding that young children construct knowledge by continually observing and testing hypotheses based on concrete experiences. Unlike older students and adults, they are not yet able to mentally manipulate objects.

When teachers link technology use directly with hands-on activities, children can test their hypotheses in more than one way. This has been demonstrated in several studies. In one, children who used developmental software in conjunction with other concrete activities showed greater gains than did children who used the software alone, or who did not have access to the software (Haugland 1992).

Foreman observed that when young children use manipulative materials in conjunction with computer simulations of the same materials they develop spatial/mathematical concepts sooner than if they use either manipulative materials or computer simulations alone (1985). In playing with an electronic version of blocks, students were able to replay the last few events before the blocks fell and figure out a different way to create the buildings. With real blocks, similar reflection could only be achieved when block-building was videotaped and replayed. At ages four and five, children focused more on process when using the computer and more on outcome when using real objects. Foreman believes that the focus on process in the computer setting was related to the ability of the program to replay a sequence of events. The replay function allowed the children to reflect on what had happened by seeing it again.

One of the most valuable uses of computers is to help children document and record their observations of the concrete world. Documenting is by nature abstract, whether children do it by drawing, by writing with a pencil, or by using computer tools such as word processing and digital images.

> *Computers limit the social interaction that builds language and conceptual development.*

Instructional strategies, not computers, determine social interaction. Child psychologists generally agree that collaboration among children supports increases in conceptual development. From a Piagetian point of view, disagreement between students as they work on a problem together causes *disequilibrium* in their cognitive structures (Crook 1987). Students move to higher levels of concept development as they naturally strive to regain equilibrium. From the Vygotskian point of view, children can support each others' learning in the "zone of proximal development." Therefore,

> *Teachers need to consider how to structure computer activities to encourage collaboration at the computer. Learning then comes from two sources— interaction with peers and interaction with the technology.*

teachers need to consider how to structure computer activities to encourage collaboration at the computer.

Figure 1.2. Interaction Between Students Working at the Computer Is Important to Their Development

---

Scaffolding for learning then comes from two sources, interaction with peers and interaction with the technology. Ekebland and Lindstrom (1995) observed young children collaborate in playing computer games involving quantification. The children supplied adequate verbal and modeling clues to help each other learn. These findings are consistent with other research with children three years of age and older (Crook 1987).

Computers limit creativity.

The issue here is not computers, but how they are used. Teachers who would not normally use worksheets with young children often use drill and practice software that is essentially an electronic workbook (Haugland and Shade 1994; Van Hoorn, Nourot, Scales, and Alward 1999). Although computers are efficient for rote learning, for young children the emphasis on this form of learning can increase anxiety about getting the right answer and result in creativity loss (Haugland 1992). While young children often enjoy drill-and-practice software, its effects need to be considered (Shade 1994). Researchers have reported that young children using drill-and-practice software tend to become less collaborative, more competitive, and more dependent on the teacher, while those using open-ended software tend to develop problem-solving skills (Clements and Nastasi 1992). Therefore, if drill-and-practice software is used at all, it needs to be used very judiciously.

The primary use of computers should be to support children in their creative work. Research studies have shown that when developmentally appropriate open-ended software is used, young children have greater gains on a variety of developmental measures (Haugland 1992) and develop greater self-esteem (Clements, Nastasi, and Swaminathan 1993).

The National Association for the Education of Young Children Position on Technology

In 1996, the National Association for the Education of Young Children (NAEYC) published a position statement on technology based on the research available at that time. The following is a summary of the NAEYC position:

- ♦ When they choose and use technology, teachers should apply the principles of developmentally appropriate practices in the same ways as they do with other classroom activities.

- ♦ Teachers should integrate technology as one of many options available to young children in the learning environment.

- ♦ Teachers should work to ensure that all children, including children with special needs, have equal access to technology.

- ♦ Teachers should avoid software that includes stereotypes or violence, especially if the child controls the violence. Software choices, like other materials, should reflect the diversity of today's world.

- ♦ Teachers should work with parents to choose appropriate software both for school and home use.

- ♦ Teachers should use technology in their own professional development (for example, e-mail to collaborate with other teachers, the Internet to retrieve educational resources).

An introductory note to the position statement states that the word *technology* is used primarily to refer to *computers and children's software* but that the position logically extends to telecommunications and multimedia. The focus on software reflects the research to date, which mostly identifies the characteristics of educational software that are developmentally appropriate and that lead to growth.

Technology Tools: Issues Related to Young Learners

When teachers use technology tools with young children, some special issues need to be considered:

♦ Is the use that the technology supports appropriate to this grade level?

♦ Does the technology provide the support that allows the use to be appropriate earlier than it might otherwise be?

♦ Is the software design and interface simple and intuitive enough for children to use?

Is the Use That the Technology Supports Appropriate to This Grade Level?

The issue of appropriate content is fundamentally important; it is a core issue of curriculum design for young children. Whether on or off the computer, children should be working with content that is appropriate to their stage of cognitive development.

> *The issue of appropriate content is fundamentally important. Whether on or off the computer, children should be working with content that is appropriate to their stage of cognitive development.*

According to Piaget, one characteristic of the pre-operational stage of development (roughly ages two to seven) is that children have not yet mastered concepts of quantification. During this time, meaningful math experiences help children see the relationship between numerals (written symbols) and objects. One such activity might be to count objects and represent symbols of these objects in a pictograph. The correspondence between the physical objects and the symbols helps students understand simple graphing. It is important that this connection not be lost in the desire to integrate technology.

Some Internet projects that have been published on the Web and used with students as young as kindergarten require them to collect data and submit it to appear on a Web site graph, where an adult combines it with data from other classes. In response to these projects, the child development specialists I interviewed repeatedly said that children at this age would not make meaning from the spreadsheet, although they might find it interesting to see their data appear on a Web site and know that other classes had done the same work. The connection between the physical experience of counting objects and the graph that represents these objects gets lost when data from several classes are combined, or when someone outside the classroom does the graphing.

A popular Internet project that is used very successfully with upper elementary students demonstrates the issue of firsthand experience. In one variation of this project, children in several different classes across the country open bags of M&Ms and sort and count them by color. They then submit the data to a spreadsheet via the Internet. The data is graphed and shared in order to answer questions that students pose or that are raised by the project coordinator. A third grade class might want to know whether all the bags have the same number of each color. A fifth grade class might want to know how much variation existed for each color.

What meaning might this activity have to a kindergartner or first-grader if it were used at this level? Certainly, the first part of this activity is hands-on and highly motivating. If the children do not eat the candy first, they can determine whether or not there are the same number of each color in their class's package. Children would get practice in counting and sorting, although the sorting categories are predetermined by the project. They might also take great pride in seeing their data on the Internet.

Because of their limited experience with charts and graphs and their emerging numerical literacy, they would probably do better to develop charts and graphs within the classroom where they could see firsthand the relationship between the numbers in the chart and the M&Ms. In this case, the children can make the concrete connection only to the part of the chart that their class entered. The problem here lies not in the design of the unit, nor in the use of the technology, but in the age appropriateness of the project when it is used with students in the pre-operational stage of development (see Chapter 10).

Does the Technology Provide the Support That Allows the Use to Be Appropriate Earlier Than It Might Otherwise Be?

Vygotsky's theories point out that adults and more capable peers can support children in their learning at a point just beyond what they can do by themselves, in what he calls the *zone of proximal development* (see Chapter 10). Many researchers and supporters of technology in schools have theorized that technology can support learning in the zone of proximal development, much as human mentors do (Solomon 1986; Haugland and Wright 1997).

Haugland and Wright describe *Kid Cad* as a good example of tool software that provides scaffolding. Designed for children ages seven and older, *Kid Cad* allows students to explore perspective and architectural design. Often, perspective is taught beginning in the third grade (about age eight) but children find it is harder to draw objects in perspective than it is to understand the concept. *Kid Cad* helps children carry out their design ideas and experience changing perspective without the difficulties that drawing by hand present. Other examples of tool software that provide scaffolding are talking word processors that read children's writing aloud, writing programs that provide prompts, and drawing programs that allow children to accurately draw basic geometric shapes.

Is the Software Design and Interface Simple and Intuitive Enough for Children to Use?

> *When children can understand the use of the technology and that use is valuable to them, we should not deprive them of those tools just because it takes mediation from an adult or older child to give young children access.*

Ideally, we want to use technology tools that children can master so that their attention is on their work and not on the tool. There are some tools, such as writing programs, that have been specifically designed for young children. These are likely to have such features as colorful interfaces, simple menus, built-in illustrations, built-in drawing tools, and synthesized speech. Some examples of highly rated writing programs that are designed for young children are *The Amazing Writing Machine, Kid Works Deluxe,* and *Storybook Weaver Deluxe* (California Instructional Technology Clearinghouse 1998; Haugland and Wright 1997). In choosing a program, look for one that is similar enough to what children will use later so that the knowledge they develop will transfer to other programs. It's best to make software decisions collaboratively at the school or district level, so that children do not need to learn new software every time they move from one classroom to another.

Unfortunately many tools that are potentially valuable to young children have interfaces designed for adults. When children can understand the use of the technology and that use is valuable to them, we should not deprive them of those tools just because it takes mediation from an adult or older child to give young children access.

For example, Manuel, a first-grader, was proud of a painting he had made and wanted to take it home to his family. He had told his teacher an elaborate story about the painting, and she saw immediately that it would be a good base from which Manuel could formulate a written story. She asked him if he would like to make a computer copy of the painting with the scanner and write the story on the computer.

In the school that Manuel attends, fifth grade technology mentors, children with a high level of skill in using computer technology, assist younger children in tasks such as scanning and using software. By modeling the use of the technology, older children and adults send a message that computer tools are important tools that grown-ups use too, and that the young child's work is important enough to warrant a grown-up's tool.

We should view these tools much as we view other tools that we model or help children to use, such as an encyclopedia, a dictionary, a hammer, or a ruler. In each case, the purpose of the tool is the focus, not the ability of the child to use the tool without help. Adults and older children can model the use of the tool and mentor the child's use until the child can take over. Technology, when used as a tool, is no different.

A Closer Look at Technology Integration: The Experience of the Education First Sites

In the course of the three-year Education First demonstration the way in which many of its participants thought about integrating technology across the curriculum changed significantly. Participants were teachers, technology coordinators, principals, the Education for the Future staff that supported the schools in whole-school change and technology integration, and the Pacific Bell Education First team that supported the schools with technical assistance and training. My personal role, as an Education for the Future associate, was to assist teachers to develop and write technology-infused instructional units.

Of the ten schools chosen to be Education First demonstration sites, three were elementary schools. In all three, each class had one or two computers with Internet access, and the school had videoconferencing access.

Figure 1.3. Teachers Should Model and Support the Use of Technology Tools until Children Can Take over on Their Own

With videoconferencing in particular, creating tight connections to the curriculum was difficult at first, as we looked for ways to use this exciting tool. At the time, there were far fewer distant sites that had videoconferencing capabilities than there are today. It was hard to resist the temptation to be something like a team of carpenters who had just discovered an electric drill for the first time and were looking for places to make holes! In the beginning, a few teachers, mostly at the upper grade level, did develop some wonderful instructional units that were directly connected to the curriculum. The connections were never quite as good, nor the uses as valuable, when people thought of creative activities first and then looked for the curricular ties.

Many schools found that as they worked to integrate technology well, they really needed to step back and think about their beliefs as a community. What was their vision for teaching and learning, and how could technology help them get to the vision? What did they, as a whole school, want for all of their students, and how could they develop a continuum of learning so that all children could be successful? How could technology help students be successful learners?

Once these big-picture issues were clear, we developed a planning tool to apply technology that focused attention on the curricular objectives. The planning tool involved leading teachers through the list of questions that appears below.

Integrating Technology into the Curriculum

♦ Curricular Content
- What is the curricular content?
- How does this content connect to state and local frameworks?

♦ Standards and Assessment
- What do you want students to know and be able to do by the end of the unit?
- How will you know they can do it?

♦ Instruction
- What existing instructional unit will you enhance with technology, or what instructional unit will you create to support these learning objectives?
- What instructional strategies will be used?
- What activities will students do to meet the learning objectives of this unit?

♦ Effective Integration
- What technology tools will children use in this unit that will challenge them and support their learning?
- How will these technology tools be used?

We asked technology coordinators and teachers to work together to answer these questions, and worked along with them when we were asked to do so. As teachers developed instructional units using this planning tool and tested their units in their classrooms, the most successful units at each school were published on the school Web site. Some of these units are included as examples in this book. Others can be viewed on the Web sites listed in Appendix B.

Technology, Visions, and Dreams

Virtually all literature on technology and school reform confirms the experience of the Education First demonstration school staffs. Technology, in and of itself, does not improve schools. High-quality schools have certain common elements: a clear vision, a common philosophy about teaching and learning, high standards that are known by all, consistent use of instructional strategies designed to meet students' needs, and a schoolwide plan and commitment to achieve the school's purpose. In this context, technology can:

- ◆ Provide students with tools to approach learning in ways that help them go beyond what they might otherwise have achieved.
- ◆ Provide access to the curriculum for many students who are not successful with more traditional approaches.
- ◆ Allow students to see teachers as learners.
- ◆ Provide the impetus for teachers to embrace new methods.
- ◆ Support a project-based approach to learning.

It is in this context that efforts to use technology tools appropriately with young children will be most rewarding.

Summary

The issue is not whether or not technology should be used with young children, but how it should be used. Open-ended tools can support learning and development when they are used appropriately, applying the same basic criteria as would be used in designing other activities. Technology tools such as cameras, word processors, and multimedia software make it possible for children to tell their stories using written words, images, sounds, and motion. Communication tools such as the Internet, e-mail, and videoconferencing allow them to communicate their ideas to an audience as specific as a partner or as broad as the entire world. Teachers who are knowledgeable about both the capabilities of technology tools and child development can guide the learning of young children in a way that can be stimulating and extremely effective.

References

Barnes, B.J. and S. Hill. (1983). Should young children work with computers: LOGO before Lego? *The Computing Teacher* 10 (9): 11–14.

California Instructional Technology Clearinghouse. (1998). http://clearinghouse.k12.ca.us/

Clements, D.H. (1994). The uniqueness of the computer as a learning tool: Insights from research and practice. In *Young children: Active learners in a technological age,* edited by June L. Wright and Daniel D. Shade. Washington, D.C.: National Association for the Education of Young Children.

Clements, D.H., B.K. Nastasi, and S. Swaminathan. (1993). Young children and computers: Crossroads and directions from research. *Young Children* 48 (2): 56–64.

Clements, D.H. and B.K. Nastasi. (1992). Computers and early childhood education. In *Advances in school psychology: Preschool and early childhood treatment directions,* edited by M. Ettinger, S.N. Elliot, and T.R. Kratochwill. Hillsdale, N.J.: Lawrence Erlbaum.

Crook, C. (1987). Computers in the classroom: Defining a social context. In *Computers, cognition and development: Issues for psychology and education,* edited by J.C. Rutkowska and C. Crook. New York: John Wiley & Sons.

Cuffaro, H.K. (1984). Microcomputers in education: Why is earlier better? *Teachers College Record* 85(4): 559–68.

Ekebland, E. and B. Lindstrom. (1995). Collaboration as pedagogy, collaboration as window. In *CSCL '95: Proceeds of the first international conference on computer support for collaborative learning,* edited by J.L. Schnase and E. L. Cunnius. Mahwah, N.J.: Lawrence Erlbaum.

Foreman, G. (1985). The value of kinetic print in computer graphics for young children. In *Children and computers,* edited by E. Klein. San Francisco: Jossey-Bass.

Hampton, C. (1998). Unpublished interview.

Haugland, S.W. (1992). The effect of computer software on preschool developmental gains. *Journal of Computing in Childhood Education* 3 (1): 13–30.

Haugland, S.W. and D.D. Shade. (1994). Early childhood computer software. *Journal of Computing in Childhood Education* 5 (1): 83–92.

Haugland, S. and J. Wright. (1997). *Young children and technology: A world of discovery.* Needham Heights, Mass.: Allyn and Bacon.

Kostelnik, M.J. (1993). Developmentally appropriate programs. ERIC Digest. ED356101 93.

National Association for the Education of Young Children. (1996). Position statement: Technology and young children, ages three through eight. *Young Children* 51 (6): 11–16.

Shade, D.D. (1994). Computers and young children: Software types, social contexts, gender, age and emotional responses. *Journal of Computing in Early Childhood Education* 5 (2): 177–209.

Solomon, C. (1986). *Computer environments for children: A reflection on theories of learning and education.* Cambridge, Mass.: MIT Press.

Van Hoorn, J., P.M. Nourot, B. Scales, and K.R. Alward. (1999). *Play at the center of the curriculum.* 2nd ed. New York: Merrill.

2

Graphic Images

Albert Einstein is universally recognized as the preeminent example of the scientific genius. That scholars should explore Einstein's writing and interviews for clues of his cognitive processes is therefore no surprise. What they have uncovered, however is a surprise to many. Einstein reported that he first worked out his ideas as "more or less clear images."

G. Speedel and M. Troy, 1985

The idea of using photos, paintings, and drawings as part of children's work is hardly a new idea to teachers. Children read picture books long before they read written words. They tell wonderful stories about their drawings long before the rest of us can recognize what these drawings represent. Drawn images as a form of documentation have a role in human experience that goes back to prehistoric times. To ignore the importance of images would be to deprive children of one of the most important tools with which they organize their thinking and language development.

Figure 2.1. Drawn Images Have an Important Role in Human Experience

Teachers have been using photographic images in one form or another for many years. Polaroid cameras, video cameras, and now digital cameras have all had a part in making it easier to capture children's work in graphic form. The power of images to document children's work and to support children's thinking and development, can be seen in this story told by Patricia Nourot, professor of education at Sonoma State University in Rohnert Park, California:

> When I was a graduate student, I became quite interested in how children develop a sense of self, and used videotaping with my preschool class to explore this topic. I spent quite a bit of time observing children as they watched themselves in videos I had taken of their play.

> One day, Molly and I were watching a tape that showed her playing house with two other children in the dramatic play area. She was the mother, baking cupcakes. She mixed the batter, poured it in the pans, put it in the oven, then asked her family what they wanted to drink with the cupcakes.

> As we watched, she was horrified to see that she had failed to close the oven door! She reached out to the screen, expecting to reenter the scene to close the door. She was startled when her hand hit the screen, and then she turned to me, paused, and said, "Patricia, you can never go back!" Here is an example of a child's construction of time and space that occurred as a result of the use of video.

By using digital graphics, teachers are finding it increasingly easy to regularly incorporate images to help children reflect, observe, document, and write. Digital graphics as computerized files provide the ability to:

- ◆ Take photos at very little cost.
- ◆ Give students access to files of class photos that stay organized.
- ◆ Allow students to use the same photo many times.
- ◆ Save children's artwork without taking up classroom space.
- ◆ Allow children to take their artwork home and keep a copy in class for future use.
- ◆ Change the size of children's artwork to use for greeting cards, post cards, and other creative work.
- ◆ Make modifications, such as cropping pictures.

Photographs

Putting Children in Control

Many teachers see the value of using photographic images, but widespread use of cameras is still not common. In most schools, photos are taken at special events and occasionally to document work, and cameras almost always are kept in the hands of the teacher or a trusted adult. Teachers may see the value of putting cameras in the hands of children and giving them control of the documenting process, but also are keenly aware of the barriers, which include:

◆ Cost

◆ Time lapse in developing film

◆ Equipment breakage

All of these concerns are answered, or will soon be answered, by digital cameras.

Cost of film and developing is a real issue when using traditional cameras. Children must take many pictures to have a few that tell a story well. Teachers know that it is unreasonable to put a camera in the hands of a young child and then prevent the child from using it enough to gain skill and judgment about what pictures to take. It may seem easier and kinder to avoid the problem by taking the pictures for the child. Even then, teachers often must pay for the film and development themselves or deplete their very limited budget for classroom expenses. Digital cameras are still expensive to buy, but their price is dropping rapidly and there are no operating costs for film or development.

The time lag in developing traditional film can be a deterrent to taking pictures, especially when immediate feedback is the goal. In the past few decades, Polaroid cameras have been one solution, but the cost of film is relatively high. Digital cameras address both the time lag and cost of film. Photos are downloaded to a computer and can then be used immediately in student work; there is no time lag between taking the picture and being able to use it. Images can be printed on a black and white or color printer that is connected to a classroom computer.

Fear of breakage is another reason that teachers keep control of cameras rather than put them in the hands of students. Interestingly, the four interview participants who are most knowledgeable about preschool children all believe that young children can learn to be careful with equipment, given the right training and context. When sturdy, low-cost digital cameras become available in the near future, we will still want to teach children to be careful with equipment, but the stakes will be much lower.

What the Future Holds

We are on the verge of a major shift in photographic technology that is as significant as the shift from adding machines to hand calculators that occurred in the 1970s. In 1998, sturdy, low-cost digital cameras designed for children's use appeared on the market. The same year, a *Consumer Reports* test of digital cameras noted that "the results of our tests were surprisingly good." Digital camera quality is improving, and the cost is falling to the point were it will soon be possible to provide children with cameras whenever they want to use them in the course of their work. "Digital cameras allow children to save what they want, and get rid of the rest without using up anything, simply resolving the issue of waste" (Hakansson 1998).

> *We are on the verge of a major shift in photographic technology that is as significant as the shift from adding machines to hand calculators that occurred in the 1970s.*

Getting Started

Most teachers currently have a single camera in the classroom—usually their own. Even with one camera, it is possible to use photography closely in connection with student work.

Figure 2.2. Young Children Can Learn to Take Care of Cameras in the Classroom

You can get started by:

♦ Keeping a loaded camera in your desk or closet.

♦ Taking pictures of children working on everyday projects, not just of special events.

♦ Inviting children to take pictures under your supervision.

♦ Letting children know that when they are doing important work, they can ask to take a picture.

♦ Fundraising for film, while you advocate for a digital camera!

Photographic Images versus Drawing and Painting

As long as taking photos in the classroom was costly, teachers relied almost exclusively on children's drawings to provide images in conjunction with student work. Now, teachers have more choice about when to encourage children to use photography, when to continue to encourage children to draw or paint, and when to use a combination of documenting processes.

The primary consideration is the purpose of the image. Is the image intended as:

♦ The child's artistic expression?

♦ Documentation of an observation?

♦ The record of an event?

♦ The record of work that cannot be saved?

Artistic expression and documentation are very different processes, yet they are often assumed to be the same.

Because most primary grade children cannot yet draw accurately, their drawings alone don't provide a detailed record for the purpose of recording and documenting observations and events. When teachers ask young children to draw a picture of what they observed without photos or support for learning to draw, they inadvertently set up their students for failure and for the resulting lack of self-confidence. When I visit classrooms, I am shocked to find so many second and third grade children who are already convinced that they cannot draw well.

> *It makes sense to encourage young children to draw when creativity is desired and to use photographs and video images to supplement drawing when accuracy is important.*

It makes sense to encourage young children to draw when creativity is desired and to use photographs and video images to supplement drawing when accuracy is important. Somewhere around the third grade, most children begin to include considerable detail in their drawing and have developed the necessary hand-eye coordination to document accurately. In the meantime, teachers can help students develop the most important drawing skill—that of observation. As children develop skill in drawing and learn various forms of diagraming (third to fourth grade and beyond), drawing becomes more useful as the sole way to document observations.

Using Photographs to Improve Written and Oral Language

Learning to communicate well orally and in writing is one of the most important benchmarks of success in the primary grades. Children who have learned these skills have learned how to:

- ◆ Observe and document.
- ◆ Organize ideas in sequence.
- ◆ Use descriptive language.
- ◆ Move from oral to written forms of communication.

These communication skills are known to be connected to higher order thinking skills in general, and therefore affect every aspect of a child's success in school.

Many of the teachers I have observed and interviewed believe that writing flows from pictures, and that pictures actually trigger language and help children organize their thoughts. Although this may be true for older learners as well, it is especially noticeable in young children who cannot yet use other tools such as outlining to lay out an organizational structure for their writing.

Photos are an excellent way to document observations, especially in the area of science (Baldi 1997; Cochran 1998). Children reconstruct in their minds the steps that they followed in their work, and what they observed.

One second grade teacher described how digital photography improved this common experiment:

> As in the past, we began the project by discussing the different things that plants need to grow: sunlight, soil and water. Then the children planted beans in three plastic cups. One cup was put in the light and watered three times a week. One was put

in the light, but watered only once a week. One was put in a closet, and watered three times a week. Every Friday, the children measured the plants.

This year, for the first time, we photographed the plants, scanned the photos, and put them in a folder (computer file) so that the children could use the photos in their writing. The children were able to compare the photos that had been taken each week and see the progress of growth more clearly for each of the plants. At the end of six weeks, each child had created a log of the weekly observations from which to draw conclusions. I found that children's observations were more in-depth with the photos, and that sequencing and retelling their observations was facilitated. An added benefit was the delight that children and parents had in the finished product.

Rosa H.

Everyone I interviewed noted that using digital photos with word-processed text motivated their students. Students feel very important when they do what grownups do and when their work looks like grown-up work. Even when children's own artwork is scanned, the product has a professional look.

Many teachers have begun to use digital images to help children develop the sequencing skills necessary for storytelling. In an interview, Linda Koistinen, media center specialist at Haight School in Alameda, California, described the use of digital cameras to help children retell events:

Teachers now take either a digital camera or video camera to record highlights as they engage their classes in walking excursions in the neighborhood or in other activities that will be the basis for writing. The images are used to help children think about formulating their writing using a "beginning, middle, and end" structure for their stories. The photos are used as a prompt to help children sequence their ideas. Images also help students recapture rich details and put them into words. Pre-writers may need to dictate their stories to an older child or adult, although many second and third graders will be able to move from the oral description to written form on their own.

Moving from Image to Text

In the process described above, children develop a story that begins with photos. Knowing how to choose photographs to illustrate a story that has already been written is much more difficult, and is not at all intuitive to young children. It takes a great deal of experience, and perhaps a level of reasoning that most young children do not yet have (Hampton 1998). It is far more natural for children to start from a photo and create a story about it, than to write a story and then choose an appropriate picture.

Photos are a way to take home work that can't normally go home, pointed out Jane Baldi, school reform coordinator at Paden School in Alameda, California. In programs that are developmentally appropriate, much of children's work at the lower grades is concrete and experiential; children need graphic forms of documentation to reflect and write about these experiences. Writing flows naturally from photos at the primary level, especially when children are writing to their parents or other people they care about (Baldi 1997). The value children take away from these experiences can be deepened through a process of multiple forms of "representation" (Nourot 1998).

Figure 2.3. A Student Documents His Classmates' Documentation Process

Although the process will be different in each instance, the following is one example of a documentation sequence:

- Students record an experience using photos and audiotaping.
- From these, students retell, discuss, and interpret the experience.
- Students document the experience through art and writing.
- Students write about their experience, using their art and photos to help them organize their writing.
- Students discuss how they documented their experience, and document the processes they have used.
- The teacher displays the various forms of representation together.

I have observed many fine teachers use similar processes successfully in their classrooms:

> Today I observed Mel's second grade class studying light and shadows. A few days ago, they measured their shadows at the beginning of the day, at lunchtime, and before they left the school. They also photographed their shadows at various times of day, and outlined their shadows on the schoolyard with chalk.
>
> Today they are experimenting with shadow puppets to try to develop some hypotheses about what makes the shadow change size and shape. Mel has been videotaping four students as they "play" with the shadow puppets. Afterwards, as they discuss the changes in the shadows they observed, he suggests that they replay certain parts of the videotape. He encourages their thinking with questions like, "What do you see happening in this section of the tape?" and "Why do you think the shadow grew larger at that moment?"
>
> The children have some ideas, and they want to review the tape again "to see if that's the way it really happened." After recess, they will write about their ideas using the photos and video for support.
>
> Author's journal 1996

Through many forms of representation and documentation, children clarify their thinking, develop new concepts, and develop written and oral language skills. This approach, which has been adapted from schools in Reggio Emilia, Italy, is discussed briefly at the end of the chapter.

Other Ways to Use Photographic Images

Sequencing

Students put photos they have taken in sequential order. Determining the order of the pictures leads students to describing what happened in the sequence, both orally and in writing. Using student-generated photos ensures student interest in the subject and ensures that the material will be culturally relevant to the student.

Pattern Repetition

The concept of repeated patterns underlies much of mathematical and scientific thinking. Patterns can be observed in nature or can be created with manipulative objects. When children make patterns using beads or other manipulative objects, their patterns can be photographed and stored in digital form as a graphic file. Students can then use the pictures of their classmates' patterns to recreate and repeat the pattern, using the same manipulatives.

Phonics

Students photograph objects that contain phonetic sounds appropriate to their reading level. Children in the same class might create a book of sounds together, with each child or small group photographing objects with different sounds. The pictures and words can then be made into a book or multimedia presentation.

Oral Language Development

As children act out stories, they are videotaped. They then review the videotape, asking, "Did the story make sense? Did the action happen in the right order?" When action is important, such as in a play, video captures that action better than still photography. As in the example about studying shadows, the videotape becomes the organizer from which writing occurs.

Story and Play Writing

Using a video capture program, individual frames from the video activity above can be made into graphic images and saved to use like any other still picture to encourage student writing. At the second and third grade level, small groups of children can write their plays using the graphic images to trigger memory of the events. Each child in the group can take home a copy of the group's work, because the pictures and text are printable computer files.

Documenting Science and Math Observations

Digital or scanned photos are used as part of journal writing in science and math to record "what we did" and/or "what we observed." The process is essentially the same as for the earlier example in which students were studying light and shadows. When used in this way, photography supports literacy as well as observation, documentation, and reflection.

Exploring Family and Community

The core concept of the social studies curriculum in the early grades is the idea of family and community—the child's relationship to others. Teachers have long used photography to supplement children's writing about their families and their explorations of the different cultures in their classroom. Digital photos, either scanned or taken with a digital camera, allow children to use their pictures more than once and to produce results that look professional.

Some teachers have worked with their students to create multimedia class albums of children's writing, photos, and voices that reflect the cultures of the families in their class. (See Chapter 4 for more information.)

Drawings and Paintings

Drawing on a Computer

A variety of software programs, from paint programs to word processing programs to multimedia programs, now have built-in drawing and painting functions. This is true of programs designed for business use, home use, and use by children. It is almost impossible to find a computer that does not have drawing tools in one program or another. Drawing and painting functions have valuable uses, but freehand drawing is one of the most difficult to master.

Creating Digital Photographic Images

◆ Traditional Cameras and Scanners

Developed pictures can be scanned using a color scanner attached to a computer and saved as digital graphics directly to the computer. Because students generally don't work on the computer that is connected to the scanner, they must move their graphics using a floppy disk or other storage device, or through a network.

◆ Digital Cameras

Digital cameras save images directly in digital form. Some cameras save images on a special disk or a regular floppy disk; others require that you download images to the computer using a cable provided with the camera. Cameras with liquid crystal displays (LCDs) are useful to help you decide which images to keep and to sort graphic images taken by children into their own folder of work on the computer.

◆ Video Cameras, Video Capture Software, and a VCR

A VCR can be attached to a computer that has audiovisual capability (as do most Macs and many PCs). You can play videotapes on the VCR, display them on the computer screen, and record them in digital form either as QuickTime movies or as single frames, by using a video capture program. Because QuickTime movies require large amounts of disk memory, the common practice is to make them very short or to save individual frames instead.

Most adults find drawing with a mouse quite frustrating and difficult. Often children have the same reaction, although there are some who enjoy the challenge of using a mouse as a drawing tool. Several companies make art tablets that use a pencil-like drawing tool. This comes closer to the real experience of drawing, but still is difficult because one must look at the screen where the drawing appears rather than at the tool that is producing the drawing. In an interview, Burke Cochran of the School of Education and the Center for Teaching and Professional Development at Sonoma State University pointed out a central problem: in young children, whose hand-eye coordination is not yet strong, drawing in one place (the mouse pad or the art tablet) while viewing the drawing in another (the screen) adds one more impediment to their drawing (1998).

For the purpose of artistic expression, drawing and painting with real art materials still is easiest for most children, yet exposing children to creating art on the computer provides them with one more tool that they can use at their discretion.

Exploring Geometry with Drawing and Painting Tools

Teachers find drawing and painting tools quite valuable for providing young children with the opportunity to explore the properties of geometric shapes in the context of play. Unlike drawing freehand on computers, perfectly formed shapes are very easy to construct using drawing tools.

For example, children can see the new shapes that occur when geometric shapes overlap. Once overlapping shapes are created, the fill tool (paint bucket icon) can be used to fill in each closed space in a different color that highlights the new shapes that have been created. The fill tool is also useful for understanding the difference between open and closed forms, because the "paint" spills out of open forms onto the rest of the picture.

Clip Art

Many software programs come with a variety of clip art that children can learn to bring into their pictures. In some, these are viewed as stamps, which makes the connection for children to a tool they already know. Clip art should not be confused with children's creative artwork, but it is a very useful tool to help children learn to sort, categorize, make patterns, and learn many other skills and concepts appropriate to their age and development (Hampton 1998).

Categorizing with Clip Art

Programs that allow clip art to be placed easily and quickly are especially useful for categorizing and sorting activities in which children want to choose many different objects for their work. At the beginning, the teacher may suggest categories, but children will quickly catch on and think of their own. Figure 2.4 shows the work of two kindergarten students who worked together on categorizing.

Using clip art for categorizing is much faster than drawing the items or cutting and pasting. Therefore, children are able to focus more of their time and effort on working with the concept of categorizing. Children enjoy guessing each other's categories. Once the idea of playing this sort of game with the computer is known by students, they will find their own ways to challenge each other's thinking.

Figure 2.4. Categorizing Clip Art with Kidpix Studio

Supporting Phonemic Awareness and Phonics with Clip Art

Clip art allows children to easily make books that chronicle their progress as they learn phonetic sounds. In contrast to workbooks, the products the children make reflects their choices in graphic images and design. They therefore have a much greater stake in their work.

As children are first learning to distinguish between phonetic sounds, an appropriate task would be:

Make a page with all the pictures you can find that start like the fish. (An adult would then help the children label the pictures.)

A beginning reader might work on the following task:

For each long vowel sound, make a page with pictures that have that sound and label your pictures.

Clip Art Frames with Repeated Patterns

Earlier, photos were discussed as a way to document patterns made with concrete objects. Children can also explore pattern repetition working together or alone with the stamps in the software program *Kidpix Studio*. One teacher suggests creating frames for children's original work by using the stamps to make repeated patterns. For example, a child might write a poem about taking a family trip and then decorate a frame for the poem with a repeated pattern of cars and hills.

Scanned Art Work

Every child should have a rich variety of experiences using real art materials in the primary school years. One would hope that this would continue into the upper grades, but among young children, art has a special place because:

- ♦ Art helps develop small motor skills.
- ♦ Art is a form of expression that does not require the ability to read and write.
- ♦ Art can help to develop literacy by providing material to write about that is important to the child.

Young children love to make books, greeting cards, and gifts for their families by combining their artwork with their written messages. Scanning allows children to take home their original pictures and keep copies at school, too, to use whenever they want in connection with their writing. It also allows artwork to easily be resized as illustrations in books or greeting cards.

Creating Greeting Cards

Students can use their scanned artwork with their writing to create greeting cards. Any word processing software that allows graphics to be imported will work for this purpose. Cards made in this way have the look of professionally made cards, although they are truly the child's own work. Students can also use photos in the same way.

Telling Stories and Writing Books

Scanning children's artwork and encouraging them to write about or dictate their stories using a computer enables them to create work that looks very much like a real book. Very young children will need the help of an adult or older child, but even by the end of the first grade, a few children will master the processes of importing a scanned image into a word processing program and writing their stories. Using scanned images with word processing gives children the sense that they have done something very important, which indeed they have. It's not that the computer makes the work important, but that the computer makes the work *look* important in the children's eyes, which is a powerful motivator.

Scanning Children's Art Work

Scanning is only slightly more difficult than using a photocopier, and works in much the same way, except that the copy is saved as a graphic file on a computer attached to the scanner.

- ♦ Place the item face down on the scanner bed.*
- ♦ Prescan the item to show it on the computer screen.
- ♦ Select the area to be scanned.
- ♦ Scan the picture.
- ♦ Save the picture. The format that you choose for saving (for example, PICT, JPEG, or GIF) will depend upon the software program into which you will bring the picture. Check the software manual for directions.

*A flatbed scanner is preferable to a sheet-fed scanner, especially if the artwork has paint that might peel or flake off. It also provides the option of scanning pictures from books.

A Closer Look at Documenting: The Reggio Emilia Approach

This chapter has explored many ways for children to use graphic images, especially in the area of documentation. It is almost impossible to read about the ways in which children in Reggio Emilia, Italy, learn to document their work, without re-thinking our own processes. In these schools, panels that cover the walls document the learning process with such elements as photos of original experiences, children's artwork and writing about these experiences, and photos of children creating their documentation. This multilevel documentation provides the scaffolding for both teachers and students to reflect and learn from their work (Hendrick 1997).

Using this approach, very young children develop skill at documenting their work through drawing and painting. Although the drawings are typical of children in terms of hand-eye coordination, the ability of the children to capture detailed observations is quite striking. Teachers gently guide their students to develop drawing and observation skills by allowing them time to draw the same object many times and by discussing their observations, much as art teachers in the United States do with older students.

In *Bringing Reggio Emilia Home,* Caldwell (1997, p. 73) describes the reaction of her American colleagues as she began implementing this strategy with four-year-olds:

> The teachers also seemed skeptical about the idea of suggesting that children draw "from life" or from looking at something specific. Again, they were concerned that this request was asking too much of young children. I thought of Vea, who helped me understand that she did not want to rush children along, only to offer them the possibility of making relationships between their marks and their experience. If they were ready, they would make the connections, which would be *their* connections. If they were not ready, they wouldn't.

Some may dismiss the teaching strategies of Reggio Emilia, pointing to the differences between our schools and theirs. The schools are designed for children up to age six, there is a full-time art teacher to assist children in documentation, and clearly the schools are well supported. Nevertheless, there is a great deal of knowledge about teaching and learning to be gained from studying this system.

Grade-Level Guidelines for Using Cameras, Video, and Scanning Equipment

When should children be allowed or encouraged to handle cameras, videocameras, and other technical equipment? The answer will vary tremendously from child to child. The child's coordination, interest, and willingness to care for the equipment will all play a part.

Activity	Approximate Grade Level	Considerations
Students use photos taken by the teacher.	All grades	Teachers model use of cameras as a tool for documenting, organizing, and thinking about ideas.
Students take pictures using digital or standard point-and-shoot cameras.	All grades	Teacher must set the expectation that children are responsible to take care of cameras and other breakable objects. Initially, supervision is needed.
Students assist teachers in using scanners.	Grades 1 to 3	Modeling use of scanners sends the message that these are valuable tools for "grownup" work. Scanning is not difficult, but there are several procedural steps that must occur in sequence. Many children will need support into the fourth grade.
Students import pictures into word processing or multimedia programs.	Grades 2 to 3	Students will need help in organizing graphic files so that they can find the picture that they want to import.
Students operate video cameras using a sturdy tripod.	Grades 2 to 3	Some teachers have found that even younger children can operate video cameras and care for the equipment.
Students learn to edit digital photos and scanned artwork.	Grades 3 to 4	Students can learn to crop, darken, and lighten images. More extensive and purposeful editing is generally saved for older children.
Students operate a handheld video camera.	Grades 4 to 6 and above	Children have difficulty understanding the relationship between their own movements and the movements shown by the camera.

Summary

Technology tools that are available today can capture the important images that come from children's experiences and make them available for children to use as they think about and communicate their ideas. Advances in digital camera technology are making it possible for students to take pictures themselves and then use them as organizers for their writing.

Photographs and clip art are also useful for teaching concepts and skills such as categorizing, pattern repetition, and phonics. Graphic images help children think about science explorations and social studies concepts by allowing children to document hands-on experiences in a way that encourages reflection and representation. When children's artwork is scanned or created on the computer, children can make professional-looking greeting cards and books to share with their families. Children love using these tools, and are delighted by the quality of the work they can produce.

References

Baldi, J. (1997). Unpublished interview.

Caldwell, L.B. (1997). *Bringing Reggio Emilia home: An innovative approach to early childhood education.* New York: Teachers College Press.

Cochran, B. (1998). Unpublished interview.

Consumer Reports. (1998). Snapshots: Time to go digital? *Consumer Reports* 63 (11): 30–34.

Hakansson, J. (1998). Unpublished interview.

Hampton, C. (1998). Unpublished interview.

Hendrick, J., ed. (1997). *First steps toward teaching the Reggio way.* Upper Saddle River, N.J.: Prentice Hall.

Nourot, P. (1998). Unpublished interview.

Speedel, G. and M. Troy. (1985). The ebb and flow of mental imagery in education. In *Imagery in education: Imagery in the educational process,* edited by A. Sheikh and K. Sheikh. Farmingdale, N.Y.: Baywood Publishing Company.

3

Word Processing
and Literacy

The computer allows the young child the ability to create letters, words, and stories long before their own muscle coordination allows them to create clear DeNealian letters using the old tool, a pencil.

Jean Casey, 1997

Chapter 2 explored the use of graphic images to support emerging language, literacy, and conceptual development. Throughout that chapter, there is an underlying assumption that word processing is also a tool that young students will use in putting words together with images, yet this assumption is far from universally held in schools. Even when primary teachers see the value of word processing, they are often pressured by their upper grade colleagues not to introduce it unless they first teach keyboarding, so that children won't "form bad habits." Unfortunately, the keyboarding debate too often overshadows what word processing has to offer students as they are becoming fluent writers.

Word processing offers young children:

♦ A way to get ideas in print even if forming letters with a pencil is still very slow and difficult.

♦ The ability to produce text that looks like grownup work.

♦ A way to correct mistakes, rethink ideas, and revise without recopying.

♦ The potential to collaborate easily with a partner in the writing process.

♦ Choice in how to write, when added as an additional tool to paper and pencil.

♦ Text-to-speech capability, in which the computer reads the child's writing aloud.

Although this book focuses primarily on more recently available tools—graphics, multimedia, e-mail, the Internet, and videoconferencing—this brief chapter provides a look at the research on word processing and its use as a tool.

Beginning to Write with a Word Processor

Teachers often notice that young children like to write using the computer. Researchers have consistently found that young children

Researchers have consistently found that young children not only enjoy writing, but write more, write more fluently, and revise their work more when they use computers.

not only enjoy writing, but write more, write more fluently, and revise their work more when they use computers. (Bowman and Beyer 1994; Clements 1994; Strickland, Feeley, and Wepner 1987). These phenomena have been observed in a variety of different settings, including one in which I was personally involved. At the Education for the Future sites, Victoria Bernhardt conducted student surveys to find out about attitudes toward and experiences with e-mail, the Internet, and videoconferencing (1998). Because availability of networked computers varied, some classes took the surveys on the computers, while others used paper-and-pencil versions. The surveys were given to all students from third grade up, and to second-graders at some of the schools. Across the board, we noticed that the children wrote more on the open-ended questions when they took the surveys on the computers, and that their responses were clearer and more detailed. This was true for the second- and third-graders as well as for older students. We had not set out to explore the value of word processing and at that time, we were not familiar with the previous research in this area. Yet the differences were striking enough to notice without looking for them.

Figure 3.1. A First Grade Student Shares Her Writing With Her Brother

Fine Motor Skills and Writing

I am visiting the first grade class where I have two e-mail buddies, Alisha and Mikey. I have been reading and responding to their messages for some time, but this is the first time that I have visited their class and watched them compose a message to me. They think it is great fun to show off their skills, and I promise to respond as soon as I get back to my computer. The first thing I notice is how slow their keyboarding seems to me. I'm surprised that they don't seem to be frustrated by the pace. As I look up from the computer, I notice two children writing a story together at a table a few feet away. Their handwriting is at least as slow and laborious. Now, one is erasing a mistake so hard that he is scrubbing a hole in the paper, making his partner very angry. Mikey's voice brings me back to the task at hand. "Is that right?" he asks, pointing to a misspelled word. We sound it out together and he corrects it without a trace of the error remaining.

Author's journal, Spring 1997

Cochran-Smith, Kahn, and Paris (1988) found that word processing can free young children from the constraints imposed by their difficulty with handwriting and allow them to focus more on the content of their writing. They also noted that young children often find learning how to word process to be less frustrating than do older children. While they become familiar with the keyboard, they take about the same time to hunt for a letter as they do to produce the letter by hand. At first, older students are somewhat frustrated by the additional time it takes to compose using the keyboard because they are already proficient with paper and pencil. They need to develop greater computer skills to catch up to their writing skill level.

Cochran-Smith, Kahn, and Paris suggest that while older children are learning the mechanics of word processing for the first time they should initially work from a written draft rather than compose simultaneously. Kindergartners and first graders need to know less about word processing to get started because their writing skills are also at a beginning level. Except for the most basic computer skills, they can learn word processing informally, in the context of exploration, at the same time that they are developing other writing skills.

Keyboarding

Most K–1 teachers I talk to believe that the keyboard is a help rather than a hindrance in their students' writing. At about the third grade, teachers tell me that the lack of keyboarding skills is a real impediment to children's writing if they haven't had much previous experience with keyboarding. However, this observation should not lead to the conclusion that children should be taught formal keyboarding early.

The same fine motor coordination issues that make it difficult for young children to write make teaching formal keyboarding inappropriate at the K–1 level. In the interviews I conducted, a consistent point of view was expressed:

- Children should use a keyboard as soon as they are interested—in preschool if they want to.

- Children tend to learn the placement of the keys informally as they write at the pre-K–2 level, as long as they are taught the basics (delete, return, shift, space, etc.).

- Access to keyboarding games is useful because it helps familiarize children with the placement of the keys.

- When fine motor coordination is no longer an issue, somewhere around third grade, more formal keyboarding should be introduced.

- Starting at about the third grade, some formal keyboarding instruction should be provided each year.

- The purpose of teaching keyboarding is to help students obtain a speed that can support the writing process—about 25 words per minute.

- It is not in the interest of students to withhold use of the computer until they obtain a specific level of keyboarding speed.

> *Learning keyboarding does not have to be an obstacle to writing on a computer; teaching keyboarding does not have to be a burden at any one grade level. Keyboarding, like other skills, builds through use over time.*

Learning keyboarding does not have to be an obstacle to writing on a computer; teaching keyboarding does not have to be a burden at any one grade level. Keyboarding, like other skills, builds through use over time. Perhaps the root of the keyboarding debate is tied to past experience. The typing class that so many women teachers were expected to take in high school is not a good model for teaching keyboarding to young children. A chance visit to

Laura Sangalli's second/third grade class at Paden School pointed out that children can enjoy learning to type.

It is nearly time for school to dismiss. Laura is
working with four children, reviewing the progress
of their group's work. Another six children are
reading books in pairs on the rug. There are many
activities going on at this moment; the children are
clearly using their time productively right to the
end of the day. At several tables, children are typing
as fast as they can on small, plastic keyboards. They
stare intently at a one-line display as their small fin-
gers hammer away. This particular typing tutor—
there are many others as well —is called *TypeRight
II*. What is most impressive is the speed and skill
that these children have obtained, even though they
don't touch-type. The children have learned several
strategies, partly from the teacher and partly on
their own. They use both hands on the appropriate
sides of the keyboard, and a thumb for the space
bar. As words appear on the screen, the children
type them and they disappear. Every two minutes,
the number of successful strokes is displayed. The
children are trying to surpass their own personal
best score.

After school, Laura explains that she started out
teaching formal lessons in keyboarding, but the students resisted. Once she let the students take control, their keyboarding speed increased and it became fun. Now, many children type at least twenty
words a minute, and some type faster than forty!
However, Laura is quick to point out that her students see the connection between what is essentially
drill and practice in keyboarding and their ability to
use a keyboard to write. Students in her class regularly use the computer for authentic work.

Revising

"Do I have to copy it again?" Every teacher who has taught
the writing process is familiar with these words. Word processing
supports the writing process at all ages because it frees students
from laboriously recopying revisions. *Writing as a process* is consistent with the theories of both Piaget and Vygotsky (Daiute
1988). This approach gives students considerable control over

Figure 3.2. The Student is Intent on Beating His Own Record for Speed and Accuracy

their writing and allows them to use inventive (more appropriately called phonetic) spelling and other nonstandard conventions to discover writing until their skill level develops.

If teachers want students to look reflectively at their writing and try to improve it, it is important to give them the tools that make revising personally rewarding instead of painful. A 1992 multinational study found that the most common use of word processing was not for revising, but for recopying final versions of handwritten work! (Grunberg and Summers, reported by Downes and Fatouros 1996). Of course, classrooms often don't have enough computers for children to use, which may, in part, account for these findings.

Some schools are turning to small portable word processors to solve the problem of access. These tools solve many problems when they are used well:

- ◆ They are relatively inexpensive.
- ◆ They use a rechargeable battery.
- ◆ They are lightweight and sturdy.
- ◆ Some are available in class sets with a station for charging the batteries.

♦ Student work downloads easily to a computer to be used with other programs (e.g., for including graphic images).

For older students, these tools have a serious downside—they show only a small amount of text at a time, often no more than a few lines. For students who are writing long essays, this is a major drawback. On the other hand, for young children who only write a few lines of text at a time, they are ideal.

Cooperative Learning and Collaboration in the Writing Process

Collaboration is a key component of teaching writing as a process, especially for young children who are developing oral language skills at the same time that they are learning to write. Despite the trend toward an emphasis on discrete writing components—spelling, punctuation, and grammar—written language depends on oral language skills, which depend on human interaction. As children discuss their ideas in the process of writing, they are building the conceptual base and the language skills that will make them better writers.

Figure 3.3. First Grade Students Collaborate as They Compose an E-mail Message

Daiute found that second graders were able to collaborate more easily in their writing using word processing rather than paper and pencil. From a Vygotskian approach, the conversation that goes on between partners during writing is then internalized and added to the knowledge base of the students (Daiute 1988). Other researchers have observed that the public nature of the computer screen encourages students to help each other correct and refine their work (Silvern 1988).

The computer provides another advantage when children collaborate in the writing process—it allows partners to share equally in the pride of their work. Handwritten work looks like it belongs to only one child, and only one child can bring the original work home. Word-processed writing can be taken home by each partner.

When Computers Talk Back

Nina is sitting at my Macintosh laptop computer in the library of her school. She is four-and-a-half years old, one of the youngest students in her kindergarten class. She types a string of letters and tells me that she is writing a story. I ask her if she would like the computer to read it to her. She watches me highlight the letters and select "speak selection" from the tools menu. She laughs with glee as the computer voice pronounces, "slifmefmaemf."

We do this several times, changing the voice on the computer. This produces more laughter, until Nina has an idea. "Let's hear it say my name," she says as she starts to search for the N. After some effort, she has typed her name—the only word Nina currently knows how to write.

Now the computer says, "Nina." Nina's laughter turns to sheer joy. "I'm going to change the voice," she tells me. She has obviously been watching me because she now knows how to do it even though she can't read the tools menu. After several replays of her name, she wants to try my name. She is already thinking about the words she will write.

This is Nina's first experience with a speech synthesizer, and my second. I have borrowed Nina from her class to try it because I do not dare suggest a tool to teachers until I see how it works with kids. I am pleased and so is Nina.

Author's journal, Fall 1997

In Nina's classroom, the text-to-speech feature of the computer has become a favorite in the writing center. Children use it in a variety of ways that they have discovered themselves. Sometimes they sound out the words they want to write; at other times, they copy words from favorite books or from the words posted on objects around the room. The feedback they get by hearing the words pronounced seems to be helping them become writers and readers.

Jean Casey's book *Early Literacy: The Empowerment of Technology* (1997) includes a thorough review of the research about how text-to-speech technology encourages early literacy, including substantial research of her own. Although studies that rely solely on norm-referenced test scores have been inconclusive, Dr. Casey's work in six California school districts to evaluate *Writing to Read*, an IBM text-to-speech software program, used a variety of measures and found substantial gains in writing and reading fluency. An evaluation of twenty-seven schools in Mississippi that used *Writing to Read* and a pilot study of schools in Juneau, Alaska, that used the software reported similar gains. Numerous other studies reported in the book reach similar conclusions. These research findings make enormous sense when one thinks about how easily a computer can provide auditory feedback on demand, which helps students associate oral expression with written words.

Speech synthesizers help students:

- *Learn to spell phonetically.* Until students master standard spelling, we want them to sound out words as well as they can. Phonetically incorrect spelling sounds strange when pronounced by speech synthesizers.

- *Learn words by sight as well as phonetically.* The child sees words as the computer reads them. Words inevitably become part of the child's sight vocabulary as they are written, spoken, and seen together, over and over.

- *Correct their own writing.* When the computer reads a child's writing aloud, the errors become obvious. For example, the computer voice will not pause at the end of a sentence unless there is a period and the new sentence starts with a capital letter.

◆ *Put their ideas into writing at a younger age than was thought possible.* Once children begin to associate letters with sounds, they can start to put their ideas on paper with the help of a speech synthesizer. Where students have been dictating their stories to an adult, many can now use a word processor instead (Casey 1997).

◆ *Develop left-right directionality.* When children write on a computer, the letters always appear from left to right, reinforcing the conventions of written English (Cohen 1997).

Casey believes that text-to-speech technology bridges many of the debates about teaching strategies by putting the student in charge, thereby moving the focus to learning strategies. In particular, it bridges the phonics/whole language debate. With the support of text-to-speech, children use phonics, whole language, and the combination of the many approaches that work best for them, leaving the argument to the adults in the faculty room.

Grade-Level Guidelines
for Word Processing

Word processing is very appropriate for young children to use as they are developing oral and written language skills.

Activity	Approximate Grade Level	Considerations
Students learn to use a mouse and to use basic menu options (open, cut, copy, paste, print, save, quit).	Pre-K to K	Many preschool children can master this.
Students learn basic keyboard commands (shift, delete, space, return, caps lock, arrow keys).	Pre-K to K	Many preschool children can master this.
Students type letters and copy words. They use text-to-speech to hear their writing.	Pre-K to K	Text-to-speech gives auditory feedback to help students learn to sound out words.
Students "hunt and peck" to write their ideas, using inventive (phonetic) spelling. They use text-to-speech to hear their writing.	Grades K to 3	By third grade students will be able to write quite well using computers if they have used them for several years.
Students play keyboarding games to learn letter locations.	Grades 2 to 3 and above	Keyboarding games require good eye-hand coordination.
Students are formally taught keyboarding skills.	Grades 2 to 3 and above	Keyboarding games require good eye-hand coordination.

Summary

Young children generally write more and write more fluently when they use a computer. Word processing helps them with the writing process in a variety of ways. Very young children and children of all ages with hand-eye coordination difficulties find typing on a keyboard less difficult than forming letters with a pencil. Because children are able to correct mistakes without having to recopy their work, they are more willing to revise and improve their writing. Collaboration between students in the writing process is facilitated by word processing, because the children involved can have equal ownership. The result is writing that is of higher quality and looks more grownup.

Text-to-speech technology, a feature available in many computers and programs, helps students to learn to write phonetically while they acquire the conventions of spelling. It gives students immediate feedback so that they can correct their mistakes. Students are therefore able to begin writing their ideas without dictating at an earlier age than they otherwise could.

References

Bernhardt, V.L. (1998). Education First demonstrates success with technology. *ASCD Curriculum / Technology Quarterly* (Winter) 8 (2), 5–6.

Bowman, B.T. and E.R. Beyer. (1994). Thoughts on technology and early childhood education. In *Young children: Active learners in a technological age*, edited by J.L. Wright and D.D. Shade. Washington, D.C.: National Association for the Education of Young Children.

Casey, J.M. (1997). *Early literacy: The empowerment of technology*. Englewood, Colo.: Libraries Unlimited.

Cohen, R. (1997). The discovery of written language in the computer age. In *Early literacy: The empowerment of technology*, edited by J.M. Casey. Englewood, Colo.: Libraries Unlimited.

Clements, D.H. (1994). The uniqueness of the computer as a learning tool: Insights from research and practice. In *Young children: Active learners in a technological age,* edited by J.L. Wright and D.D. Shade. Washington, D.C.: National Association for the Education of Young Children.

Cochran-Smith, M., J. Kahn, and C. Paris. (1988). When word processors come into the classroom. In *Writing with computers in the early grades,* edited by J.L. Hoot and S.B. Silvern. New York: Teachers College Press.

Daiute, C. (1988). The early development of writing abilities. In *Writing with computers in the early grades,* edited by J.L. Hoot and S.B. Silvern. New York: Teachers College Press.

Downes, T. and C. Fatouros. (1995). *Learning in an electronic world: Computers and the language arts classroom.* Portsmouth, N.H.: Heinemann.

Silvern, S.B. (1988). Word processing in the writing process. In *Writing with computers in the early grades,* edited by J.L. Hoot and S.B. Silvern. New York: Teachers College Press.

Strickland, D.S., J.T. Feeley, and S.B. Wepner. (1987). *Using computers in the teaching of reading.* New York: Teachers College Press.

Multimedia Presentations: Putting the Pieces Together

In principle, the younger the children, the more important it is that most of the activities provided for them engage their intellects. As children grow, they become better able to address routine and repetitive academic tasks because they can more easily comprehend the need for drill and practice to attain skill proficiency. Teachers throughout the early years tend to overestimate children academically and underestimate them intellectually.

Lilian Katz and Sylvia C. Chard, 1992

So far, we have discussed using graphics images and word processing together to combine images with children's writing. This combination provides a springboard for children's thinking and improves written and oral language skills. The children's work that results—pictures with text—is conceptually the same as the work that children have often done in the past, except that when children have the support of the computer as a tool the quality of their writing often improves and the product often looks more appealing to them. Although this is highly motivating, it does not change the nature of the child's actual work.

By creating multimedia presentations, students as young as four or five years old can use digital photos, videotaping, and recorded sound in conjunction with their writing to create "mind images"—pictures painted with words, sound, image, and movement—that have personal meaning, evoke emotions, and motivate children to be learners (Hakansson 1998).

The picture in Figure 4.1 was created by five-year-old Cindy using *Kidpix Studio*, after she had seen the movie *Peter Pan*. What makes Cindy's multimedia representation of Tinkerbell different from the picture shown here on paper is that the electronic version includes the sound of Cindy clapping as loudly as she can. As is often the case, this young child was not able to capture her emotions very well in the drawing or writing sample, yet the sound in her project portrays her feelings well.

Multimedia technology is a different way to communicate ideas than is traditional text. In classrooms where teachers are trying to incorporate Howard Gardner's theory of multiple intelligences (1983), multimedia is an excellent option. The following are examples of how multimedia projects can support learning through the intelligences (Armstrong 1994):

- Linguistic—written text
- Musical or linguistic—sound
- Spatial—illustrations, screen design
- Interpersonal—collaboration between students
- Bodily kinesthetic—video segments

Figure 4.1. Cindy's Representation of Tinkerbell

Clap your hands.
What Is Multimedia?

Technically, multimedia technology refers to a computer environment that includes any two or more of the following: text, graphics, sound, animation, and video. Many word processing programs allow students to incorporate pictures, and so fit into the technical definition. Functionally, however, these programs are very much like traditional text; when the work is printed it looks like the pages in a book. For discussion purposes here, the term *multimedia technology* is used to refer to programs that include at least sound, text, and graphics. Figure 4.2 highlights the differences between traditional text and multimedia.

**Figure 4.2. Comparison of
Traditional Text and Multimedia**

Traditional Text	Multimedia
Linear in format	Usually nonlinear; uses buttons to navigate
Uses text alone, or text and graphics	Can use text, graphics, sound and animation
Text-dependent; text passages are generally long	Depends on all elements; text passages are generally short
Visual communication	Visual and auditory communication
Often created individually	Often created collaboratively

Communicating ideas using multimedia technology is ideally suited to children who are not yet able to write several paragraphs on a topic. Each screen—or card, as they are usually called—captures a part of the child's work. The segments are connected using navigational buttons. The total project is broken into small chunks, which allows children to work on the various parts in whatever order they choose; it also allows many children to work together on the same project.

Most teachers are familiar with commercially prepared multimedia programs. Both CD-ROMs and Web sites use this form of interactive technology, in which clicking on buttons and hypertext leads the user from one area to another. What surprises many people is that young children, from preschoolers up, can participate in creating highly interactive multimedia projects.

Class Projects

Barbara Scales, of the University of California's Harold E. Jones Child Study Center in Berkeley, believes that multimedia technology provides a valuable way for children to work together to make something that is socially important (1997). As each child participates in creating a piece of the whole, the project helps cement the bonds of group membership. For example:

> Each child might create a card by finding a picture of an object or animal, creating a collage with the picture and scanning it, and then dictating or writing a sentence about his or her work. Each child might then record suitable sounds, such as the sound that the object or animal makes, with some adult mediation. An adult would then link together the individual children's work into a single, whole-class, multimedia project. All of the children could enjoy and participate in this group-building experience by using the presentation that they created together, and at the same time learn to recognize common words by reading each other's segments.

> Discovering oneself as an important member of the group is a central feature of socialization to the classroom, and was joyously expressed by one young child who, upon recognition of her own contribution to such a group project, cried in elation, "It's me, it's me!" Along more academic lines, the teacher might add a "read to me" button to allow nonreaders to hear a recording of the teacher. (Scales 1997)

This same process can be used by K–3 classes, adapted to their curriculum content. Multimedia technology is such a flexible tool that it is valuable for any content area in which the communication of ideas is important.

Figure 4.3. Students Take Pride in the Multimedia Projects They Create

Consider this idea, created by a first grade teacher:

At the Fall Open House, I photographed the children with their families. I wanted to find a way to tie the individual photos together to represent the connection between the students in the class. Then I had an idea. I made a main menu by scanning my class picture and putting an invisible button on each child's image. Clicking on a child in the class picture navigated to the child's individual card. The children then added their family photo and wrote a few sentences about their families.

When the class began this project, I had no idea of the importance it would take on. The final project was so much bigger than the sum of the parts. I was as surprised as the students were at the quality of our common work. In almost no time, every child could read every other child's card, or had memorized the words. Whenever a parent came to class, our class multimedia album was the first thing that the children would show.

Elaine G.

Navigating

At the kindergarten and first grade level, students generally work together on class projects, or create single screen projects that combine one picture with words and sound. Second and third graders are often ready to create several screens or *cards*. The one part of multimedia that is quite difficult for young children to manage is creating the navigational system that connects sections of work, especially if the work is more than two cards long. Creating the navigational buttons is difficult for two reasons:

One first grade teacher created a main menu by scanning her class picture and putting an invisible button on each child's image.

- ♦ The interface on most programs requires that students follow several steps that are not always intuitive.

- ♦ Even if children learn the process of creating buttons, creating a navigational framework requires abstract thinking because the framework itself is invisible.

The teacher can resolve this problem by providing a flexible template with navigational buttons, which still allows children to keep control over their projects.

For example, at the second grade level and beyond children might be working on retelling a story with a beginning, middle, and end as represented in Figure 4.4. The teacher would create a template for a multimedia presentation that has a main menu card (screen) with three buttons linked to three cards: a beginning card, a middle card, and an end card. Children would then add the graphics, writing, recorded voices or sounds, and possibly animation to the cards.

Figure 4.4. Template for Story with Three Cards and a Main Menu

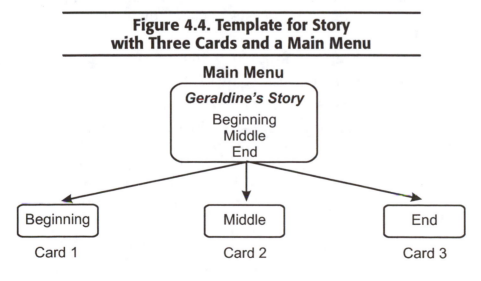

Once the teacher sets up the navigational system, it can be used again in different projects simply by changing the labels on the buttons and cards. The template that was used to create "Geraldine's Story" is the same one used in the science project on page 68.

Using Multimedia to Support the Curriculum

Oral and Written Language

The preschool farm animal project described earlier is an example of multimedia technology that supports literacy development. Children write or dictate, hear the teacher read aloud, and see the words they have written. Picture and sound become the clues that help children decode the written words. Children can choose whether to hear the teacher read or to read independently.

In the second example below, virtually all the language arts skills that are part of the primary curriculum are woven together.

Several second grade children in Rosa M.'s class created their own skit about Little Bear, patterned after the book series by Else Holmelund Minarik. Little Bear was played by a favorite stuffed animal and the children were the other characters. As they performed their skit for the class, their teacher took digital pictures.

As they looked over their pictures, the three children were so pleased by their cleverness that they wanted to make the pictures and skit into a project they could all keep. They agreed on a multimedia presentation with three sections, following the order in the skit:

- Little Bear goes to school with his brother.
- Little Bear gets scolded by the teacher.
- Little Bear's Mommy takes him home.

A *Technology Wizard*—an older student trained to assist with technology— helped the children import three of their photos onto three cards, using *Hyperstudio*. Each child then wrote the narrative for one of the cards and recorded the narrative read aloud.

As told to the author

In the example above, the children moved through the following progression:

- Listening to a story
- Creating a skit patterned after the story
- Sequencing photos
- Organizing the skit into components
- Writing descriptions of each section
- Developing a multimedia presentation

Phonics

Children can make multimedia presentations using digital pictures of objects that contain various phonetic sounds that are related to their instructional level. Children take or choose appropriate pictures, write the words, and record the spoken words. The teacher assembles the children's work into a single project that becomes part of the instructional materials available in the classroom. Projects such as this have a personal quality because they are made by the children, and they quickly become favorites.

Documenting Hands-on Science

To the great advantage of today's young children, science instruction involves much more exploration and observation than it did in the past. Children are much more likely to develop concepts from their explorations if they are given time to document and reflect upon their work. Science journals are often used for this purpose. These are usually notebooks in which children draw what they observe and write about their observations. The problem with journals is that, although teachers value them as tools to encourage higher-order thinking, parents and students don't always view them as important work. Beginning at about second grade, students can use their journals as the basis for the creation of a multimedia presentation of what they have learned.

> *Beginning at about second grade, students can use their journals as the basis for the creation of a multimedia presentation of what they have learned.*

A typical process for moving from journal writing to multimedia would be:

- Let children know ahead of time that they will be developing a multimedia project as part of a team, using their journal as the notes for the project.

- Encourage children to take photographs to document their observations.

- As they come near the end of the investigation, have each team examine the photos, journal entries, and any other documentation that exists to determine the key ideas that they discovered in the process of their observations and journal entries. Each child then develops one of the key ideas.

- Provide a navigational template with buttons to each child's cards. It is also wise to put up a visual display of the navigational system in the room, and to review it with students. This helps them see how their work fits into the whole project.

- Have each child develop one or more cards that describes a key concept or discovery, using the template provided. Provide support as necessary.

Figure 4.5 shows the navigational template that a second grade teacher provided to students for a multimedia project that documented a unit on force and matter. It is the same basic template that was used for Geraldine's story, described earlier in this chapter.

Figure 4.5. Navigational Template for "Forces on Matter" Presentation

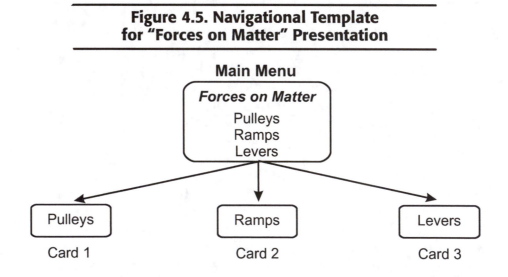

Through hands-on investigation, children explored the effect of pulleys, ramps, and levers on their ability to move heavy objects. Working in groups of three, they chose three photos to document their observation. Then, each child developed one card in the multimedia presentation, using a photo and writing a few sentences.

In this example, the teacher provided the navigational structure, but did not provide a formula for the individual cards. Generally, she tried to create as little structure as she could, while making sure that the children could be successful. However, she plans to improve the projects in future years by adding videotaping, which she feels will demonstrate the effect of force on matter better than still photography.

Exploring Family and Community

Using digital photographs to explore the family and community was suggested in Chapter 2. Judith Van Hoorn of the University of the Pacific's Benerd School of Education sees multimedia technology as a way to bring the children's families and cultures into the school, and to ensure that there are instructional materials in the classroom that reflect all children's cultures. This is especially important when children come from cultures that have not been addressed by developers of more traditional curriculum material (1997).

> *Multimedia technology allows children in a class to share their family's traditions, favorite foods, stories, and songs with each other in a way that is captured permanently and enjoyed over and over again.*

At all grade levels, multimedia class projects are a wonderful way to build a sense of community in the class while reflecting its diversity. As second and third graders become more competent readers and writers, they can also extend this work by creating their own family story albums. Multimedia technology allows children in a class to share their family's traditions, favorite foods, stories, and songs with each other in a way that is captured permanently and enjoyed over and over again.

Several years ago, Harriet R, a colleague of many years and an outstanding teacher, agreed to test a template I had developed using *Hyperstudio* for a unit on family and culture called *Family Story Albums*.

When I enter Harriet's third grade classroom, Jeanette greets me immediately. "I want to show you how much I did," she says, leading me to the computer. She has been working on her album for nearly a month, and has engaged her whole family in the project.

Jeanette directs me to click on a picture of her older brother, DeWayne, under which she has typed, "Dewayne is my big brother. He likes to tell me scary stories." When I click on DeWayne's photo, I hear Jeanette's voice imitating him with a loud "Boo!"

She next directs me to a picture of her great-grandmother. Another click of the mouse lets us hear Gram say, "I'll tell you how I tricked a bear when I was a girl, and Jeanette will write it down." This is a story that Jeanette's great-grandmother has told to two generations of children in the family. Clicking on the album tab marked *Favorite Story* brings us to Jeanette's written version of the story. It is about eight paragraphs long, and includes Jeanette's drawings and several sound effects. I am amazed by the length and complexity of the written work, and ask Jeanette how she did it. "Gram and I did it together, of course!"

Harriet is pleased with the involvement of the children's families in writing their stories, and believes that it is important for children to see adult family members modeling the writing process.

Author's journal, Spring 1996

When children write collaboratively with adult family members, they get the message that writing is an important activity. In projects such as this, the family has expertise to share with the child and the class. Children can take home paper copies of the project, while the electronic version becomes part of the class treasures. A fuller description of this unit appears at the end of this chapter.

Basic Multimedia Programs

Although it is not the intent here to endorse any particular software product, two products are so commonly used in schools that they are worth mention. Both of these products are relatively inexpensive and can be learned in an afternoon by a teacher who has basic computer skills. Both have very simple animation procedures; objects can be animated simply by dragging them across the screen.

Kidpix Studio is used successfully in preschool to upper elementary grades or older. When first grade children have access to the program over time, they can become quite competent at using most parts of the program. Menus have both pictures and words. Although the program is simple to use, it uses many standard icons and procedures that will transfer as children move on to more adult programs. Teachers report that very young children can successfully use pictures and tell a story in *Kidpix*.

Hyperstudio is widely used by children from second grade through high school. Many adults use *Hyperstudio* as well. It is intended for children who are able to read menus and simple dialogue boxes. The dialogue boxes guide the novice through the steps needed to add text, clip art, photos, sound, buttons, and animation. Some teachers tell me that second and third graders, who are still beginning readers, use clues such as beginning sounds to recall the menus and dialogue boxes. This is a highly motivating program. The current version of *Hyperstudio* allows work to be saved in HTML (hypertext markup language) for posting on the World Wide Web.

Many other multimedia programs exist that can be used with children, and new ones are appearing on the market regularly. As mentioned earlier, it is wise to make program choices as a school or district, rather than class by class, so that children can build on what they already know when they move from one class to another.

If buying software is not an option, you may already have a multimedia tool available on your computer. *PowerPoint*, part of *Microsoft Office*, is a tool for making presentations that works much like a slide show. Teachers often use it for assembling class projects, and it can be used by second and third graders with support from an older child or adult.

Getting Started

When one looks at the possibilities, it is sometimes overwhelming to imagine how to begin using multimedia technology in the classroom. On the other hand, when one looks at the possibilities it is equally impossible not to begin at all! The following are some ideas about how to get started:

◆ Spend time outside of class playing with a multimedia program. Older students are often experts, and there may be a twelve-year-old you know who would love to be your teacher for an afternoon.

◆ If students have never used a multimedia program before, begin with one of the simpler programs and allow children to explore it in the context of play for several months before they take on more formal projects.

**Figure 4.6. A Fifth Grade Technology
Mentor Helps Younger Students with
Their Multimedia Project**

- ◆ Teach a few children to use the aspects of the program that you want all children to use in the context of the project. Use an each-one-teach-one strategy whereby every student takes turns being a learner and a teacher.

- ◆ Choose a simple project for the first time that has strong ties to the core curriculum. Expect that first experiences with multimedia technology will take students longer than later experiences, just as with learning anything else new.

- ◆ If possible, recruit an older student or parent who is familiar with the multimedia software to help.

An Example Unit That Integrates Multimedia Technology

The unit that follows is one that I developed as a student in a technology class designed for teachers. It was possible to design and build the template in a three-credit course without prior experience in using a multimedia program.

Family Story Albums

Grade level: Grades 2–3 and up

A family story album is a collection of pictures, writing, and audio recordings that reflect the family's oral history, traditions, recipes, artifacts, and anything else that the family finds meaningful. Family Story Albums encourage literacy through family involvement in an area in which adult family members are experts. While the multimedia template provides a framework for assembling student work, much of the actual student work involves family members working collaboratively with their students at home. Figure 4.7 shows the template students use to assemble their projects.

Figure 4.7. Family Story Album Template Created in *Hyperstudio*

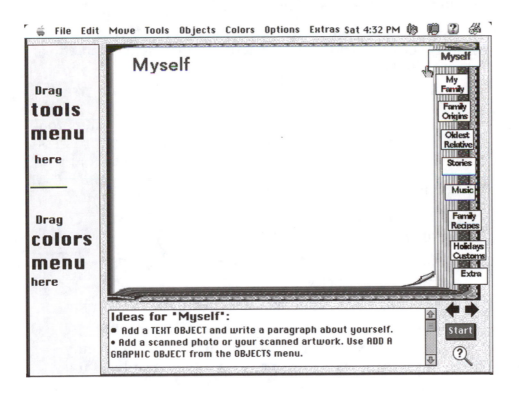

Goals

Students will expand their current knowledge about their family and culture and create in-depth presentations of their research. Through this process, they will improve literacy skills and develop an appreciation for their own and others' cultures.

Student Learning Objectives

- Students will be able to formulate questions, conduct interviews of family members, and record responses through audiotaping.
- Students writing and reading skills will improve through involvement of their families in literacy acquisition.
- Students will gain an appreciation and knowledge of their culture and the cultures of classmates.
- Students will develop computer literacy skills using multimedia design and word processing.
- Students will be motivated to expand their oral and written language skills and technology skills because of the relevancy of the subject matter.

Standards

Teachers are encouraged to check the general objectives above against their state and local standards and curricula, and adjust activities in the unit accordingly.

Assessment

Students are assessed authentically on both process and product. Teachers should use existing rubrics and standards for assessment, and familiarize students with expectations ahead of time.

Components

Each child and the teacher can decide together which of the following sections to use:

- *Myself*—The child shares personal stories with drawings and/or photos.
- *My Family*—The child describes members of his or her family and includes drawings and/or photos.
- *Family Origins*—The child describes where the family came from. Pictures, maps, or other graphics and sound may be added.
- *My Oldest Living Relative*—The child interviews, photographs, and records their oldest living relative, and decides what parts of the interview will go into the final project.
- *Stories*—Older children or an adult in the family help the child to write and illustrate a family story.

- *Music*—The child shares a brief segment from an audiotape of a traditional song sung or played by members of the family (maximum time 30 seconds).
- *Family Recipe(s)*—Children and a family member write a recipe together as they cook the child's favorite dish.
- *Family Customs and Holidays*—The child explores the customs and holidays that make their family special. The open-ended nature of the program allows children and their families to decide whether to include religious customs.

Nature of the Template

A copy of the template is made for each child, which allows the teacher to use the original again and again. The template includes:

- Hypertext menus that can be customized to include only those sections that the student or teacher selects.
- Directions for assembling the multimedia albums.
- Additional ideas for customizing the project.

For more information contact Leni von Blanckensee by e-mail at: lvonb@telis.org

Grade-Level Guidelines for Integrating Multimedia

The guidelines below are recommendations for including the components in projects with the expectation that children will continue to have assistance from an adult, older child, or peer.

Activity	Approximate Grade Level	Considerations
Students create pictures within a multimedia program and combine them with words and sound.	Pre-K to Grade 1 with help Grades 1 to 3 independently	Many first grade students are able to master this using programs designed for children.
Students import their photos or scanned artwork.	Grades 2 to 3 with help Grades 4 to 5 independently	Children can learn the procedure, but organizing and finding graphic files usually requires help.
Students add their recorded voices.	Any age with help Grades 2 to 3 independently	Children must be able to follow steps in simple dialog boxes.
Students add navigational buttons.	Grades 2 to 3 with help Grades 3 to 4 independently	Planning navigational buttons requires conceptualizing the finished work before it is completed.
Students add animation.	Any age with help Grades 3 to 4 independently	Children must learn a series of steps to add animation except in a few easier-to-learn programs.
Students add video to their projects.	Grades 2 to 4 with help Grades 5 and above independently	Video files are memory "hogs." Children must choose a very short segment from a longer video to digitize.
Students edit photographs, sound, and video for their multimedia presentations.	Grades 5 and above	Aside from simple editing such as cropping, purposeful editing requires the ability to visualize the finished product.

Summary

Multimedia projects can support oral and written language development, hands-on math and science, multicultural understanding, and just about any concepts or skills that are part of the curriculum. Multimedia technology is usually nonlinear and may include text, graphics, sound, and animation. Because of its potential to help students express their thinking while learning computer skills, multimedia technology is well worth the effort it takes to incorporate it into the curriculum.

Multimedia projects are an excellent way to incorporate multiple intelligence theory into classroom practices, and to support varying learning styles. Collaboration among students adds to the value of such projects. Children enjoy creating multimedia projects and use their creations, much like a favorite book, over and over again.

References

Armstrong, T. (1994). *Multiple intelligences in the classroom.* Alexandria, Va.: Association for Supervision and Curriculum Development.

Gardner, H. (1983). *Frames of mind: The theory of multiple intelligences.* New York: Basic Books.

Hakansson, J. (1998). Unpublished interview.

Katz, L.G. and S.C. Chard. (1992). *Engaging children's minds: The project approach.* Norwood, N.J.: Ablex Publishing Corp.

Scales, B. (1997). Unpublished interview.

Van Hoorn, J. (1997). Unpublished interview.

5

The Internet

Today, we find ourselves in the best of times, and in the worst of times. The convergence of several technologies…computers, multimedia, telecommunications on the Internet and the World Wide Web bring us quantum leaps closer to being able to deliver on the promise of technology to re-shape our entire culture. Never before have teachers had so much real potential to fully exploit the "tool" capabilities of the new technologies. We see real evidence around us every day that the World Wide Web is actually beginning to change our lives….

Today, more than ever, we need teachers who are able and willing to become side-by-side learners with their students. Teachers who are not afraid to acknowledge, "I don't know," and then can turn around and say, "Let's find out together."

Al Rogers, 1996

What role does the Internet have in the K–3 classroom? There are so many concerns about child safety and readability that teachers ask this question often. However, searching for information on the Internet is only one of its many uses, and perhaps the least appropriate Internet use for young children. The greatest value of the Internet in K–3 programs is as a communication tool and as a way of publishing young children's work.

The following are just hints of what can happen, and what is happening in schools throughout the country and the world, when the Internet is used well in primary classrooms:

♦ K–1 students at Bayview School have been watching the life cycles of moths. They have read about caterpillars, written stories about them, visited a few Internet sites selected by the teacher, and observed and documented caterpillar growth using photographs, drawings, and writing. The work of the class is documented on the Web for students and the community to see.

♦ Many third grade students in Harriet R.'s class share a favorite author. Their teacher finds that the author has a Web site. This piques the interest of the students further, and after several visits to the site and class discussions, the class sends an e-mail message to the author through her site. To the children's surprise, they receive an answer. This begins an exchange that continues through the year.

♦ Two schools in two different states that share many children of migrant farm workers now share their students' work through their Web sites. Teachers in the two schools are doing more and more projects in common, and children can see what their friends are doing while they are away.

◆ At Clinton Avenue Elementary School, a second grade unit about pumpkins is the jump-off point for poetry writing, which is published on the Web. Other classes throughout the country are invited to participate and to post the work of their students. Although student writing is the focus of this unit, it also invites teachers to share their favorite learning activities involving pumpkins, and opens the possibility of further collaboration between classes. (A full version of the unit can be found at the end of this chapter.)

Internet Analogies

It helps to think of the Internet in terms of its functions, shown in Figure 5.1, rather than as a monolithic entity of good or evil. When teachers worry about the dangers of the Internet to children, they are thinking about the Internet as a giant library, full of uncensored documents, with the possibility that children will wander unsupervised through the stacks.

Figure 5.1. Internet Analogies

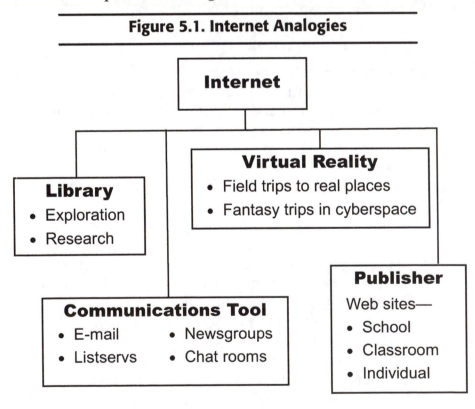

The Internet as Library

This is one of the least valuable uses for a young child, because there isn't a separate reading room just for children. If they do use the Internet to find information, they need to be closely supervised not only because of adult materials that are out there, but because most sites are focused to the interests and reading ability of older children or adults. Time spent at these sites may be entertaining—there are many pictures and animated objects—but does this use serve the child's needs or the instructional goals?

In the interviews, Millie Almy, Professor Emerita of the Graduate School of Education at the University of California at Berkeley, expressed concerns about bombarding children with images and motion through the media, especially during their formative years. This concern surfaced in several other interviews as well, but Almy in particular wondered whether children are being overstimulated and exposed to so much that it affects their ability to focus. On the other hand, she was quite enthusiastic about using e-mail and Web publishing, which puts children in control.

One way to help young children focus their attention is through a thematic or project-based curriculum. In many ways, this also addresses the issue of using the Internet as a library with young children. Nourot points out that whether children are watching television, using the Internet, or reading a book, it is the quality of the content, rather than the nature of the technology, that is the issue (1998). When teachers choose a few sites that are particularly well-suited to the needs and interests of the children in their classrooms, bookmark these sites, or actually download them onto a school computer, the Internet can be an appropriate resource.

Reminder

Before using the Internet as a library with students, make sure that your school or district has an *appropriate use policy* in place. Parents should be notified in advance of the policy, asked to review it with their child, and both the parent and child should sign the agreement.

Finding Appropriate Resources

It can take hours of searching to find a few Web sites that are appropriate for beginning readers and that connect well to a specific theme. Fortunately, there are many excellent Web sites designed for teachers where this work has already been done. They provide research links based on specific subject areas and topics, and/or are connected to specific instructional units. Some have searchable databases of links to other sites. Many of the sites note whether the links are appropriate to elementary, middle, or high school students; a smaller number distinguish between primary grades and upper elementary grades. Usually, these are the same sites that post interactive instructional units in which students are involved in using e-mail, Web publishing, and even videoconferencing. More information about finding these Web resources can be found in Chapter 8.

The Internet as Two-Way Communications Tool

Because the whole point of focusing on language development in the early grades is to improve communication skills, teachers must find meaningful contexts for children to learn these skills. The Internet can provide a real and immediate reason for children to learn to read and write when they use it to communicate with other people outside the school. The Internet as a communication tool includes:

◆ E-mail

◆ Listservs

◆ Newsgroups

◆ Chat Rooms

◆ Web sites, in some cases

Of these, e-mail can be used successfully by very young children, and Web sites can sometimes be used for two-way communication, not just for publishing. The other uses listed are more appropriate as resources for teachers.

E-mail is sent to one person, several people, or a group. Communication by e-mail isn't simultaneous, as on a phone, but it is very fast. Many teachers find that e-mail encourages and motivates children to read and write, to formulate questions well, and to learn about people from other cultures. E-mail gives children a real audience for their writing, and for their thinking and wondering. These uses are so valuable that they are addressed separately in Chapter 6.

Listservs are interest-based groups to which people subscribe. Information posted on the list is sent as e-mail to all subscribers. Listservs can be used as a teacher resource. They are convenient in that the messages come automatically, but this can also be a disadvantage. Some listservs put out so much mail that they can become a nuisance. If you sign up for a listserv, choose one that is moderated; that is, someone is responsible for screening the messages to make sure they are on topic. Don't forget to save the directions about how to unsubscribe. You can find Listservs through Internet searches, just as you would search for any other resources. However, one Web site, Liszt (http://www.liszt.com), allows the user to search for listservs by topic.

Newsgroups are also interest-based resources, like listservs, but information is posted electronically on a server, not sent directly to a subscriber. Many newsgroups are open and allow anyone to see the postings. Dejanews (http://www.dejanews.com) provides a special search engine just for newsgroups. Like listservs, newsgroups are a good resource for teachers, but are not generally useful to young students.

Chat rooms provide live simultaneous communication. Everyone who is logged onto the chat room at a given moment can "talk" to everyone else. Some Internet providers have ongoing chat rooms for their subscribers. Although these can be interesting, they are not recommended for young children. Teacher chat rooms can be valuable, but more for discussing pedagogy than for finding specific information. The exception is when a "chat" is arranged for a specific purpose. In that case, it can resemble a meeting.

Web sites, usually included in the category of Web publishing, can also be used to share the work of participants in a project. A common model, used with older students, involves classes in different locations that collect data and share it in a graph on a Web site. The teacher in charge of the project actually posts the data, but all the students are involved in collecting it and in interpreting it. The use of the Web, in this case, is more for communicating than for publishing.

The Internet as Virtual Reality

There are many places children can go on the Internet—real museums, real zoos, and even fantasy worlds. Just as in real life, some are very valuable, and others are a distraction that eats away children's time. Teachers should be highly selective in using the Internet in this way, recognizing that children need to have some context in which to understand virtual field trips. Virtual realities are meaningful when they are tied to children's real experiences, interests, and inquiries.

Several kindergarten students are building a zoo in the classroom using blocks and plastic animals. A heated debate erupts over whether the tigers belong in the same field as the zebras. One child insists that they both have stripes, so they should live together, although several others believe that the tigers might eat the zebras. They appeal to the teacher for help.

Teacher: *How could we find out the answer to this question?*

Student: *We could go to the zoo and ask someone.*

Teacher: *We don't have a bus to take us to the zoo right now, but we could visit the zoo Web site on the computer.*

As told to the author

In this case, a virtual field trip to the zoo is directly related to children's existing knowledge, experience, interest, and questions. The children in this example already have a context for understanding a virtual zoo. Visiting the zoo Web site is one way to answer the questions of these children by bringing the zoo to them.

The Internet as Publisher

When classrooms are truly places where children create original work, a logical next step is to provide a real audience for student work. Like the rest of us, children work harder when the product of their work is public. Teachers at all levels who have published the work of their students on the Internet report that children have a sense of importance and pride when they know that their work is public. Children love to watch the numbers increase on a visitor counter on their Web site long before they have a sense of what very large numbers mean. As one kindergarten student put it, "So many people want to see my frog picture!"

The Internet is the ultimate in public display, or as Joyce Hakansson, software designer and founder of Theatrix Interactive puts it, "the ultimate refrigerator door for proud relatives." Publishing work also allows classes in distant areas to work in parallel on the same projects, and to see the solutions that other children, far away, have created. One notable benefit that Web publishing provides is that it allows children to view their work from the perspective of the audience. When children see their work on the Internet, or view their work on video or through videoconferencing, they are far more able to see it objectively, reflect on its quality, and want to improve it (1998).

Figure 5.2. Students Know That Their Work Is Important When It Will Be Posted on the Class Web Site

---

Moving to Web Publishing

The purpose of a class Web site is to provide an audience for student work—to let the community and other classes share in the productive work of children that is occurring in the classroom. Teachers need not create special projects specifically for the Web. In earlier chapters, many examples were given of ways that digital graphics and multimedia can support student learning in the early grades. When children create projects using these tools, a natural next step is to post the projects on the Web for all to see. Any student work that children are proud of can be the material for Web publishing, including:

> *The purpose of a class Web site is to provide an audience for student work—to let the community and other classes share in the productive work of children that is occurring in the classroom.*

- ♦ Children's illustrated stories
- ♦ Documentation of science observations
- ♦ Poems

- Photos, drawings, writing, and other representations of student work
- Children's reflections about their work

It is now a common feature of software, from word processing to multimedia products, to allow work to be saved in HTML (hypertext markup language), the language behind the Web. Once a project is saved in HTML, posting it is not difficult with the help of a friendly Webmaster, the technology specialist in charge of a Web site. If no such person exists at your school, there are several other sources that can be of help.

A Word About Web Authoring

Turning student work into HTML for posting on a Web site is definitely not work for K–3 students, but it also is not as hard for adults as one might think. Even if you have older versions of programs that do not allow you to save work in HTML, there are simple Web authoring programs for this purpose. Once you start, you can check your work by opening your document with a Web browser such as *Netscape*. Make sure all the graphic images and other parts of your Web site are saved in the same folder.

If this seems too adventuresome to take on, and if you have no technology support at your site, contact the high school in your area. Many high schools have classes that teach Web authoring, and your site may be just the project a savvy high school student wants to take on.

Finding a Home for Your Web Site

You don't have to be a technology guru to find a home for your class on the Web. There are many sources of free space for class Web sites and free advice.

Your School District's Web Server

Many school districts have their own Web servers, a special computer that is designated for hosting the Web sites of the district and its schools. In some school districts, the teachers simply give work to be posted to the Webmaster. In other districts, the process is much more cumbersome. Check with your district to see if they supply this service in a way that meets your needs.

Nonprofit Organizations

Several organizations exist to help teachers use technology in ways that support learning. For example, the *Global Schoolnet Foundation* hosts over 3,400 school Web sites. This foundation, also known through its Web site as the *Global Schoolhouse*, has been supporting the use of the Internet to publish student work and collaborating on projects for many years. It is described further in Chapter 8, page 146.

Internet Providers

Many Internet providers now provide space on Web servers for their customers as part of the basic charge, or for a nominal additional fee. Some provide additional services free to schools. If you have an Internet account with a commercial provider, check their services.

Internet or Multimedia Software Companies

Several software companies provide free space for classroom Web sites. These are generally companies that market their software to schools.

Web Sites of Other Teachers

If you collaborate with other teachers on projects they have posted on the Web, they will often post the work of your students on their site. Although this isn't quite the same as having your own Web site, it can serve the same purpose—it creates an audience for the work of your students—and you'll need to know far less about the technology.

A Word of Warning

Although Web publishing has wonderful benefits, teachers should be careful to protect students from any remote danger associated with putting student pictures on the Web. Avoid using full-face photos in which children can be easily identified and using children's names associated with photos. Represent children through their work, rather than with their faces.

Finding Existing Projects on the Web

As just noted, an alternative way to become involved in Web publishing and Internet projects is to join one of the many projects posted on the Web. Often, teachers begin by publishing the work of their own students, then reach out to others in their school, and ultimately invite classes in other places to join their projects. If you respond to one of these invitations, the teacher sponsoring the project may post your students' work on the Web for you. On such sites, children see the work of other students along with their own as part of a bigger project. A full example of such a project, The Pumpkin Patch, designed by Susan Silverman, appears later in this chapter.

Web publishing projects are ideally suited for young children because they are one of the most simple forms of collaboration between classes. They are somewhat like parallel play; each class works on the same project separately and then shares the work students have produced.

Web publishing projects are ideally suited for young children because they are one of the most simple forms of collaboration between classes. They are somewhat like parallel play; each class works on the same project separately and then shares the work students have produced. Often, closer relationships between classes grow out of the shared project, but they are not a requirement for successful Web publishing.

A somewhat more complex model, one that involves direct communication and involvement between classes, is also possible. Many of these involve children providing data for a database or graph, an activity that is much more suited to the development of older students. A few, such as the Monster Project shown in Figure 5.3, can be appropriate to children of any age.

The Monster Project (http://www.win4ed.com/minds-eye/monster) is a highly motivating vehicle for teaching the writing process using communication between children through the Internet. At one site, a child draws an original monster and then uses descriptive language to communicate that image. Children at the distant site recreate the monster from the description. Both the original image and the recreation are posted on the Monster Project Site for children to compare. The project ties directly to language arts standards in writing, reading comprehension, and technology; teacher and student outcomes are described on the Web site (see Figure 5.4). Even for teachers with no prior experience with Internet projects, the originators of this project—Brian Maguire, Suzy Calvert, and the Maxwell Hill Gifted Center—have provided all the support that teachers need to give their students an engaging experience and a real reason to improve descriptive writing skills.

Figure 5.3. The Monster Project Web Site

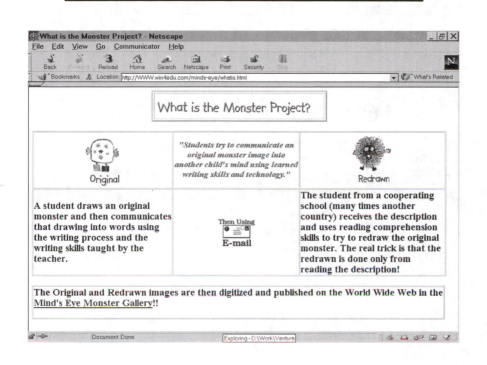

Assessing Existing Projects

In determining the value of an Internet project, consider whether it is a project that you would do with your class without an opportunity to publish on the Web or collaborate with another class. Too often, projects claim to be appropriate to K–5, but really fit the needs of students at the upper end of the range. Other projects just don't hold up to careful examination once the attraction of collaborating on the Web is put aside. The quality varies enormously. On the other hand, there are projects such as the Monster Project available in cyberspace that are so worthwhile and motivating to students that there is no reason to invent a new project by yourself.

High-quality Internet projects ideally involve activities that:

♦ Relate to the child's direct experiences.

♦ Are integrated into a standards-based curriculum through connections to other hands-on activities that support the same learning objectives.

**Figure 5.4. The Monster Project:
Teacher and Student Outcomes**

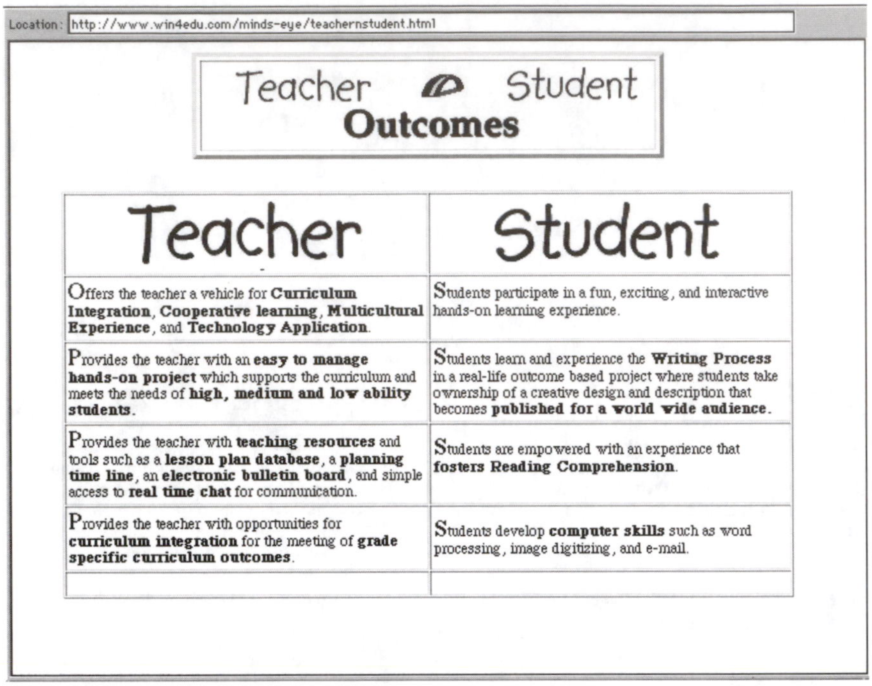

Location: http://www.win4edu.com/minds-eye/teachernstudent.html

Teacher ⟋ Student
Outcomes

Teacher	Student
Offers the teacher a vehicle for **Curriculum Integration**, **Cooperative learning**, **Multicultural Experience**, and **Technology Application**.	Students participate in a fun, exciting, and interactive hands-on learning experience.
Provides the teacher with an **easy to manage hands-on project** which supports the curriculum and meets the needs of **high, medium and low ability students**.	Students learn and experience the **Writing Process** in a real-life outcome based project where students take ownership of a creative design and description that becomes **published for a world wide audience**.
Provides the teacher with **teaching resources** and tools such as a **lesson plan database**, a **planning time line**, an **electronic bulletin board**, and simple access to **real time chat** for communication.	Students are empowered with an experience that **fosters Reading Comprehension**.
Provides the teacher with opportunities for **curriculum integration** for the meeting of **grade specific curriculum outcomes**.	Students develop **computer skills** such as word processing, image digitizing, and e-mail.

- ◆ Are interesting and challenging to students at a wide range of ability and skill levels.
- ◆ Are open-ended, allowing children to learn through their own playful investigation.
- ◆ Support language development either directly, through interactive use by children in groups, or through extensions of the activity.
- ◆ Are appropriate to children with varied learning styles.
- ◆ Can involve two or more children who are working cooperatively.
- ◆ Are sensitive to, or at least neutral about, issues of diversity and gender.
- ◆ Are accessible to students with special needs.
- ◆ Are accessible to English language learners.

Resources on the Web

Finding high-quality projects that meet your criteria is well worth the effort. There are many sources on the Web for teachers who want to use the Internet with their classes. Support generally comes from:

- ♦ State departments of education
- ♦ University education departments
- ♦ School districts
- ♦ Nonprofit educational organizations
- ♦ Corporations with educational support programs
- ♦ Commercial sites designed for education
- ♦ Individual schools and teachers

These are discussed more, with examples, in Chapter 8.

An Example Unit That Uses Web Publishing

The project described below was developed by Susan Silverman, a second grade teacher at Clinton Elementary School in Port Jefferson, New York. She listed it on the Global Schoolhouse Project Registry (http://www.gsn.org), allowing teachers to find it easily. The project is elegant in its simplicity; it builds on children's interest in pumpkins at Halloween to involve them in poetry writing, tied to hands-on experiences. The project itself and the student work it generated from many different places can be viewed at:

http://www.webcom.com/suealice/pumpkins/welcome.html

Recommended for Students: Age 6–7 (Second Graders)

Summary:

Young students will write original poems about pumpkins following an assigned format. Every child in the class will have his or her work published. In addition to the poetry each class is invited to submit some student illustrations. The illustrations may be sent electronically or by traditional mail (snail-mail). The class URL or e-mail address will be posted on the page.

Objectives:

1. Develop reading and writing skills.
2. Develop poetry appreciation.
3. Showcase student work on the World Wide Web.
4. Use the Internet for online collaboration.

This project supports the following Learning Standards for New York State:

Mathematics, Science, and Technology

- Standard 2: Information Systems

  Students will access, generate, process, and transfer information using appropriate technologies.

English Language Arts

- Standard 1: Language for Information and Understanding

  As speakers and writers, students will use oral and written language that follows the accepted conventions of the English language to acquire, interpret, apply, and transmit information.

- Standard 2: Language for Literary Response and Expression

  As speakers and writers, students will use oral and written language that follows the accepted conventions of the English language for self-expression and artistic creation.

- Standard 3: Language for Critical Analysis and Evaluation

  Students will listen, speak, read, and write for critical analysis and evaluation.

- Standard 4: Language for Social Interaction

  Students will listen, speak, read, and write for social interaction.

This project supports the following National Educational Technology Standards for grades Pre-K–2:

Standards Area 1: Basic Operations and Concepts

Standards Area 3: Productivity Tools

Standards Area 4: Communications

Standards Area 6: Technology Problem-Solving and Decision-Making

**Figure 5.5. Students Use Pumpkin Seeds
as Math Manipulatives**

Followup Activities:

1. Teachers are encouraged to share their favorite pumpkin lesson plans.
2. Children will be able to find second grade key pals or trade travel buddies.
3. Participants can add their favorite books to a pumpkin bibliography.
4. Teachers and students are invited to submit pumpkin-related Web sites to the group.
5. Children may write pumpkin poems using some of the different formats in this site and put them in their own poetry books or on other sites.
6. Participants might enjoy trading pumpkin recipes that can be made in class or at home.
7. Everyone is welcome to add his or her ideas to the list.

Project Coordinator:

Susan Silverman
susansilverman@yahoo.com
Clinton Avenue Elementary School
Port Jefferson Station, New York, 11776

Grade-Level Guidelines
for Using the Internet

The following table describes the approximate grades at which various types of Internet-related projects are appropriate.

Activity	Approximate Grade Level	Considerations
Teachers post their students' work on the Web.	All grades	Children at all ages find this motivating.
Classes in different schools use Web publishing to share the work they have done in common.	All grades	Classes are working on common projects and seeing each other's work, but not truly collaborating over distance.
Students use the Internet for exploring topics, using sites chosen by the teacher.	Grades 2 to 3	In using the Internet, a few high-quality sites should be carefully chosen and tied to the content of children's projects.
Classes in different schools use e-mail or the Web to collaborate on class projects that involve sharing descriptive information.	Grades 2 to 5 and above	Generally, collaboration over a distance is difficult and requires teacher mediation. A few projects are appropriate for second graders, but genuine collaborative work is more successful with older students.
Classes in different schools use e-mail or the Web to collaborate on class projects that involve sharing numerical data.	Grades 4 to 5 and above	Combining data collected at each site and analyzing it together via the Web is a common form of collaboration. Students must understand spreadsheets and graphs that include data collected by others.
Groups of students in different schools use e-mail or the Web to collaborate on projects (not teacher-mediated).	Grades 5 and above	Cooperative learning is difficult from a distance, even with the support of the technology.
Using multimedia tools, students assemble their work to post on Web pages.	Grades 5 and above	Students who are interested in developing advanced Web skills should be supported in their interest.

Summary

The Internet is a valuable communication tool for young children. It is highly motivating as a place for children to publish their work and to see other children's work. Two of the greatest benefits of posting work on the Internet are that it provides a real audience and it allows children to step back from their own work and view it from the perspective of the audience.

Many high-quality Internet projects already exist on the Web. When they choose, teachers should apply the same criteria that they would to other activities to determine if they are appropriate to the ways that young children learn and develop.

When a class uses sites on the Internet other than their own, adults must provide children with guidance and focus. Teachers are wise to apply the concept, *less is more,* when young children use the Internet as a library.

References

Global Schoolhouse. (1998). http://www.gsh.org

Hakansson, J. (1998). Unpublished interview.

Maguire, B. (1998). Monster Project, Windstar for Education. http://www.win4ed.com/minds-eye/monster

Nourot, P. (1998). Unpublished interview.

Rogers, A. (1996). The failure and promise of technology in education. Global Schoolhouse http://www.gsn.org/teach/articles/promise.html

Silverman, S. (1998). Pumpkin Patch. http://www.webcom.com/suealice/pumpkins/ welcome.html

6

E-mail

Most students (perhaps over 90 percent) can master what we have to teach them, and it is the task of instruction to find the means which will enable our students to master the subject under consideration. Our basic task is to determine what we mean by mastery of the subject and to search for the methods and materials which will enable the largest proportion of our students to attain such mastery.

Benjamin Bloom, 1981

Despite the emphasis modern culture places on the images, sound, and motion of electronic media, reading and writing are still the most fundamental tools for communicating, aside from speech. The Internet and e-mail are changing what we read and how we read, but not our need to read and write. Students will need to know how to write more succinctly and how to skim documents for information more quickly than their parents' generation did, if they are to survive in the information age.

Because researchers have found that children who can't read by third grade are likely to experience long-term failure in school, the pressure is on K–3 teachers to foster early literacy. Technology tools such as e-mail can help teachers support beginning and emergent readers in developmentally appropriate ways.

Why E-mail?

When young children are developing literacy, nothing is more compelling to them than getting and sending mail. Several studies have indicated that children's writing and reading skills improve when they communicate with a real audience via e-mail (Bowman and Beyer 1994). Surveys given over a three-year period at the Pacific Bell Education First demonstration sites found that teachers believe that e-mail can increase both motivation and learning (Bernhardt 1998).

Corresponding with other people gives children:

- ◆ A real audience for their writing.
- ◆ An incentive to learn to decode and understand written words.
- ◆ A sense that their work is important.
- ◆ A good way to get answers to their questions.
- ◆ A personal connection to real people outside the school.
- ◆ A way of hearing the points of view of other people.

Once schools have a network in place, e-mail has certain advantages over traditional mail (snail-mail) that makes it the method of choice for classroom use:

◆ Responses can be almost immediate.

◆ The original message comes back with the response, unless the writer intentionally deletes it.

◆ There is no postage cost or long-distance phone charge.

◆ It's easy to keep a record of the correspondence.

◆ E-mail is brief and informal and provides a good fit with the way young children write.

◆ Many busy adults, who otherwise would not have time to volunteer in schools, are willing to correspond with classes or individual children by e-mail.

◆ If the issue arises, it is easy for the teacher to monitor e-mail for inappropriate responses (a very rare problem if e-mail partners are chosen carefully).

A number of e-mail uses in the early grades support literacy development such as E-mail Buddies—ongoing relationships with other people via e-mail. E-mailing questions to experts in the area of study is also a meaningful way for children to get their questions answered. Sharing information by e-mail allows classes in different schools to collaborate on projects. In addition to writing messages, classes can send digital photos to each other as e-mail attachments. Whenever communication is appropriate with other people who are not physically in the classroom, e-mail is an excellent tool. Children can even become participants in school improvement by e-mailing suggestions to the principal.

E-mail Buddies: The Juarez-Lincoln Experience

Several years ago Nancy Camp, a first grade teacher at Juarez-Lincoln Accelerated School in San Diego, California, began matching pairs of students with adult E-mail Buddies. Her purpose was to support literacy by giving children an authentic reason to read and write, and by giving them an audience for their early writing. The staff of Education for the Future (a school partner through the Education First Demonstration Project) gladly volunteered to be adult E-mail Buddies. Two children were matched with each adult buddy so that the children could support each other's work.

Children responded to every e-mail message within a few hours. When the adult took time to respond the same day, children would often write twice. The networked computer in the classroom was set up to display a message on the screen when e-mail arrived. Nancy's philosophy is that reading and writing e-mail is important enough to allow children to leave most other activities. When e-mail arrives, children are usually free to go to the computer to respond to their buddies.

The tenacity with which children decoded messages and responded in writing amazed the most experienced teachers among us. At the end of the first year, Nancy's students had far exceeded the district standards for first grade, and had exceeded her expectations based on previous experience. After watching the enthusiasm and success of this class, several other first grade teachers joined in the project during the second year. Peg Palm, a veteran teacher with over 40 years of experience, who had initially been skeptical, became the project's greatest advocate.

> *Reading and writing e-mail is important enough to allow children to leave most other activities.*
>
> Nancy Camp

She describes the experience of her class:

> Most of my adult E-mail Buddies were from outside the educational field. The adult buddies were almost more enthusiastic than the students. Every child was teamed with a buddy. By the end of the year, eighty-five percent of my class met or exceeded the goals of the school's writing rubric for first grade. I have never seen so many children in my class write this well before.
>
> Peg Palm

Peg then went a step further and gave students an audience for their writing by creating a class Web site and publishing their work.

Advantages of Adult E-mail Buddies for Young Children

Attempts to use same-age E-mail Buddies, or Key Pals (as they are often called), were far less successful when young children were matched with other children their age. Serving the needs of beginning writers was complicated by the dictates of classroom management styles. It was difficult to find other classes that corresponded with the same regularity as do adult e-mail buddies. In classes where children were scheduled to answer their e-mail at specific times, they were only able to respond weekly or biweekly.

**Figure 6.1. Students Point to
Photos of Their E-mail Buddies**

Even more of a problem was the difficulty beginning writers had in making meaning from each other's messages. Even when the message could be deciphered, the content wasn't usually rich enough to elicit a substantial response. Observation suggested that adult buddies were a better choice for young children.

The interviews helped explain these observations. All interviewees agreed that having an adult E-mail Buddy to nurture beginning writers was highly motivating. "Buddies need to be able to facilitate the work of young children. The adult provides scaffolding for children's writing, by asking questions and modeling the format for responses " (Hakansson 1998).

The example below of an actual exchange between two first graders and their E-mail Buddy illustrates the point:

Maria and Bradley: *I hav a dog. Do you hav a dog? I hav a cat.*

Adult: *I have a dog named Bess. She has soft brown fur. Bess loves to take walks. Tell me about your pets. What are their names? What do they like to do?*

Maria and Bradley: *Brad's dog is Pesky. He is blak. He plas ball. My cat is Wisker. She is strip. She plas too. Do you have a cow?*

In this example, the children raised the topic of pets, but were not able to develop it well in their first e-mail. Once the adult responded with a description of her own pet and with some questions to help guide the response, the children were able to add much more detail in their writing. They even ended with a question—a rather funny one at that—that followed the format of the adult's previous e-mail.

Emerging writers not only need support from their buddies, they also need an audience that can continue the conversation without a substantial response (Cochran 1998). Learning to correspond with another person is much like learning to play tennis. It's a lot easier if the learner has an experienced player on the other side of the net to keep returning the ball. Although upper elementary students—fourth or fifth graders, for example—might have the writing skill to support younger students, they might well lose interest in the messages that are returned.

As children get older, they become more interested and able to write to other students their age. By the time they are in third or fourth grade, most will also have the skill to carry on a correspondence with a peer. At the same time, the curricular content gets more substantial, and many teachers feel that Key Pals should be structured around common work. Collaborative projects via the Internet, described in Chapter 5, are a natural extension to Key Pals for older students.

How to Set Up Adult E-mail Buddies

Find One Adult Buddy for Every Two Students

It's obvious that teachers need to be cautious about how they find adult E-mail Buddies for their students. Some reliable sources are:

- ♦ The teacher's own personal contacts
- ♦ Employees at the school district office
- ♦ Employees of a business that is a partner to the school (realtors, local newspapers, large corporations, etc.)
- ♦ Parents
- ♦ High school or college students, with appropriate supervision

As more high schools look for meaningful service learning opportunities for their students, mentoring young children seems a perfect match that can fill the needs of both groups of students. Successful e-mail relationships between elementary and high

Setting Up E-mail for Young Children

E-mail Programs

At this time, I'm not aware of any e-mail programs specifically designed for young children. Most classrooms use the e-mail program used by the district. You can set the preferences for larger type. Most children learn to use the reply and send functions within a short time.

E-mail Addresses

Aside from your own e-mail address, ask the network manager or your technology coordinator to set up as many e-mail addresses as there are networked computers in the class. This will allow computers to be used simultaneously for e-mail by different groups of students. Ask adult buddies to put the children's names in the subject of the e-mail.

The heading would look something like this:

From: Leni von Blanckensee <lvonb@telis.org>

To: Bonner's class <bonnerclass@district.k12.state.us>

Subject: Message to Danny and Lorine

The Address Book

Create an address in the address book for each of the people to whom children will be writing. Young children can learn to reply to an e-mail or find the name of their E-mail Buddy in the address book.

Saving E-mail

Save e-mail to a separate folder. Some teachers use a separate folder for each child; others simply move all e-mail to a single folder. The purpose is to have it available for assessment and for future reference, but in a different location from new mail.

For additional help:

- ◆ Refer to the manual or help screen for your e-mail software.
- ◆ Contact your technology coordinator or network manager for technical support.

school students depend heavily on close working relationships between the teachers on both ends.

Whenever possible, it is helpful for young children to meet their buddies in person. If that is impossible, children will at least need pictures to be able to conceptualize the writer as a real person.

Determine the Time Frame

At the first grade level, children generally begin corresponding with E-mail Buddies late in the fall or after the winter break, and continue throughout the year. Second graders might begin earlier.

Write an Introductory E-mail from the Teacher

Adult buddies need to know exactly what their role will be. Teachers should send an e-mail message that explains logistics and communicates the role of the adult in modeling writing.

Pair Students to Work Together

Two students should be matched to correspond together with one adult. In addition to the adult support, children are able to support each other if the teacher pairs children carefully. Non-writers should be paired with beginning writers, taking into consideration other factors such as oral language skills, interests, and friendships. Several teachers who were interviewed observed that tactile learners are sometimes the most sought-after partners because of their computer skills, even though they may be the weaker readers.

Begin with an E-mail from the Whole Class

Working together on the first e-mail message helps all children know the format for writing e-mail messages (that is, a greeting, a body consisting of a few sentences appropriate to the age and skills of the children, and a typed signature).

Periodically Keep Adult E-mail Buddies Informed

If the adults know what the class is studying, they can tie their conversations with students to the instructional program.

Provide Ongoing Support for Students

Think of messages to E-mail Buddies as any other writing that students do in the class. Look at student work often, encourage students to write clearly, revise, or add detail. Although there is another adult receiving the children's writing and assisting from a distance, that adult does not take the place of the teacher. Children should always maintain control over the content of their e-mail, yet have the support they need to develop their thoughts clearly.

Save the E-mails to Assess Writing Progress

The e-mails themselves can be used for authentic assessment. Teachers, parents, and the students can see how the students' writings have improved in a short period of time.

Ask the Experts:
The Mendocino Experience

In Mendocino, California, a small rural community on the northern California coast, Jessica Morton's first and second grade students study birds each year. In the course of the unit, they learn to observe, to compare, to pose questions, and to find answers through a variety of sources. One rich source of answers to children's questions has been the experts that Jessica found through Internet newsgroups. Newsgroups and listservs, described in Chapter 5, are two ways for groups of people with common interests to communicate through the Internet.

The unit reflects the teacher's hands-on approach. Students explore the world of birds through bird-watching hikes with naturalists in the area, and other concrete experiences. In the past, the teacher would guide her students through specific topics; now, she lets the interests of the students guide the unit through the questions they pose in the course of their observations. Within this student-led structure, Jessica incorporates all aspects of scientific inquiry identified in the California State Science Framework as developmentally appropriate in K–3 programs: observing, communicating, comparing, and organizing. Children also learn a great deal about the core concepts of life science, such as how animals survive by interacting with their environment and adapting to it.

Students use e-mail to communicate questions that grow out of their own observations, and that they cannot answer from direct experience or from using the many books about birds that are available in the classroom and library. Jessica has identified ornithology experts who are willing to answer her students' questions. Children learn that not all experts agree; there can be more than one answer to a question.

The following is one of several examples posted on Jessica Morton's Web page, *Birds of a Feather,* on the Mendocino Unified School District Web site (http://www.mcn.org/ed/ cur/liv/ind /birds/).

> Dear Mr. Bagwell,
>
> Haley would like to ask you a question.
>
> Why do birds lay eggs instead of having babies like we do?
>
> Thanks for your answer.
>
> Jessica Morton

> Haley,
>
> This is a very good question!
>
> An egg is basically a self-contained system which supports the developing baby bird. The baby bird which is developing inside the egg feeds off the egg yolk. The baby bird continues to grow until it is ready to break out of the egg.
>
> Mother birds can lay as many as 4 or 5 eggs over several days time. Eggs add a lot of weight to the mother bird. Just think, if she were carrying around 4 or 5 developing babies how much weight that would add to her. It would make it very hard for her to fly, and a bird that cannot fly is asking for problems.
>
> Some mother birds get the father birds to help in incubation (sitting on the eggs to keep them warm). If the mother kept the eggs inside her all the time she would not be able to let the father bird help her….

> *All the students seemed to realize and enjoy the gift we were being given: not only the excitement of frequent, sometimes almost immediate, personal answers to their questions, but the larger gift of having their "wonderings" listened to, respected, and responded to with care and skill and fascinating facts.*
>
> *Jessica Morton*

From this example, it is clear that "asking the experts" via e-mail provides students with much more than answers to questions. In fact, it has changed the nature of teaching and learning so much for Jessica Morton and her students that she has written a book, *Kids on the 'Net,* that describes the process and provides concrete suggestions for other teachers (Morton 1998).

Is E-mail with Experts Developmentally Appropriate?

"It is always developmentally appropriate to answer children's questions," asserts Millie Almy (1997). This message ran throughout the interviews conducted with child development specialists. Several pointed out the difference between providing factual information in response to children's questions and providing factual information determined by a textbook.

In the first case, children control the content of the response by their questions. Not all questions that children pose can be answered using a discovery method based on direct observation. It is unreasonable to expect children to wait years to get answers to their questions while they develop the ability to use inference. Answering their questions is therefore very appropriate, and teachers should encourage children to think about their observations, pose questions, and learn about resources to find answers.

Figure 6.2. After Reading and Discussing, Third Grade Students Formulate a Question to the Author

There is also nothing wrong with using textbooks as a resource to find answers to children's questions. It is heavy reliance on textbooks—giving children large quantities of factual information unrelated to their experience or inquiry—that is developmentally *inappropriate*.

E-mail from experts is by nature in response to students' questions, and is therefore very much related to their experience and conceptual development.

Finding and Keeping Experts

Posting a Request

Once you find newsgroups or listservs that are likely sources for volunteers to answer your students' questions (see Chapter 5), you are ready to send an e-mail request. Make sure you include the age range of your students and a clear description of the project.

Some teachers are concerned about allowing students to write to strangers who volunteer through the Internet. Most people who respond to requests from teachers are truly interested in supporting schools. Nevertheless, you should make it clear that you will be moderating the e-mail exchange.

Don't Wear Out Your Volunteers

Continue to recruit new volunteers. Responses to questions will be more thoughtful if questions to each volunteer are spread out over time. Keep a list of questions and answers that you have already received. No one wants to be asked the same questions over and over. Past questions and answers become a resource to the class.

Classroom Ambassadors: Learning About Children in Other Places

Classroom Ambassadors are stuffed animals that visit between two or more classrooms in different locations, giving children a reason to write, and at the same time, giving them an eye into the lives of children in other places. There are many variations on this project, but they all support literacy and tie into the social studies curriculum. The Classroom Ambassadors project supports many of the standards that children are expected to meet by the end of the primary grades, such as:

- ♦ Write a paragraph with a beginning, middle, and end.
- ♦ Keep a reflective journal connected to core subjects.
- ♦ Read for information.
- ♦ Understand that people come from families with different customs and cultures.
- ♦ Appreciate both the differences between people and their similarities.

Teachers can structure the project to meet other standards as well.

The Process

The originating class begins with custody of the stuffed animal. Each day, they send an e-mail to the distant class, telling about their animal that will be coming to visit soon. They then mail their stuffed animal ambassador to the distant class. Each day, the receiving class sends an e-mail to report on the ambassador's day. With kindergarten and first grade classes, this is generally a whole class activity and the ambassador stays at school. With second and third grade students, the ambassador may go home with a different child each night. If this is the case, parents should be notified ahead of time, and give permission for the "guest" to sleep over with a commitment to return it the next day, along with a journal in which the host child describes the ambassador's day. (In case of emergency, it's a good idea to have a spare ambassador in the closet.)

The ambassador goes back and forth between the two classes several times during the year, which gives children on both ends an opportunity to give and receive information. In addition, questions and answers are e-mailed as they arise, and often result in ongoing conversations between the classes.

For example, Beaver has been traveling between two schools in Alabama and California, and has been treated to various regional foods in the school cafeterias:

Class A: What does Beaver eat in your school cafeteria?

Class B: Beaver had biscuits and gravy today, but he didn't like it. We didn't like it either. We like the hotdogs better. What foods do you like to eat for lunch?

Class A: Our favorite lunches are hotdogs, cheeseburgers, and enchiladas. We never have biscuits and gravy here. Sally said that her grandma makes biscuits and gravy, but we never have them at school.

Class B: You get enchiladas at school! We like hotdogs and cheeseburgers, but we never have enchiladas. Some of the children in our class never even ate enchiladas.

Class A: Enchiladas are Mexican food. Many of the children in our class are Mexican-Americans, but everyone here eats Mexican food. Enchiladas are corn tortillas rolled up with cheese, beef, or chicken inside. They are covered with spicy tomato sauce. Jorge's mom makes the best enchiladas. We had a potluck in our school and she brought them. We are sending you a picture taken at the potluck.

As told to the author

In this case, the classes formulated the e-mail as a whole group. The teachers wanted children to know about regional foods and how these foods are influenced by the origins of the people. They were able to weave their instructional objectives into the natural conversations between the two classes that arose through their common friend Beaver, the Classroom Ambassador.

How to Find Partner Classes for E-mail Exchanges

Teachers often post variations of this and other projects on listservs or on Web sites such as the Global Schoolhouse that provide a forum for teachers' exchange. When you look for classes with which to partner several issues should be considered ahead of time:

- ♦ Do all the teachers involved have the same expectations about the time commitment to the project and the frequency of e-mail? There should be a clear commitment ahead of time.

- ♦ Do all the teachers involved have the same instructional objectives, or at least have compatible instructional objectives? Exchanges in which teachers share and support each other's instructional objectives are more likely to succeed.

- ♦ Do all the teachers involved currently have the technology in place in their classrooms to support this exchange? For example, district plans to install a network often fall behind schedule, leaving both the teacher and the partners unable to begin the project.

- ♦ Are all the teachers involved reliable? This is not easy to assess from a distance. Teachers will want to exchange e-mail several times themselves before making a commitment. If the prospective partner does not answer e-mail promptly or does not seem to have similar goals, consider finding a different partner.

Grade-Level Guidelines for Integrating E-mail into the Curriculum

When can children begin to use e-mail? The answer is very similar to when they can begin to send letters by snail-mail—as soon as they show an interest. In the guidelines below, first grade is suggested as a beginning place not because of children's developmental readiness, but because of the level of support that the teacher would need to provide if all the students were pre-readers.

Activity	Approximate Grade Level	Considerations
Classes use e-mail to share their experiences with common projects.	All grades	The value of the project is the key issue. Digital photos can be sent via e-mail, along with the message.
Students ask experts to answer their questions (teacher-mediated).	Grades 1 and above	As children move into the concrete operational stage of development, their questions become more thoughtful.
Students have adult E-mail Buddies.	Grades 1 and above	Pre-writers will dictate or work with more capable peers.
Students have peer E-mail Buddies.	Grades 3 and above	Children must be able to write somewhat fluently.
Individual students use e-mail to share information about common projects.	Grades 3 to 4 and above	Children must be able to write fluently.
Classes collaborate on projects using e-mail.	Grades 2 to 5 and above	Actual collaboration (i.e., classes working together on a single project) requires much more abstract thinking. Very few such projects are appropriate at the second grade level.

Summary

E-mail can be a real incentive for children to learn to read and write because of the personal nature of the audience. It allows even very young children to:

♦ Share their ideas with people far away.

♦ Get answers to their questions.

♦ Have a personal mentor to help them learn to write.

E-mail lets children know that their thinking and their writing is important—so important that a grown-up who is far away would answer their messages. The messages that are received create a model for children to use in their own writing.

E-mail works best to support young children's learning when they write to an adult or when they write as a whole class to another class. This gives them a partner who can provide a substantial enough response to make the exchange meaningful.

References

Almy, M. (1997). Unpublished interview.

Bernhardt, V.L. (1998). Education First demonstrates success with technology. *ASCD Curriculum/Technology Quarterly* (Winter), 18 (2), 5–6.

Bloom, B. (1981). *All our children learning: A primer for parents, teachers, and other educators.* New York: McGraw-Hill.

Bowman, B.T. and E.R. Beyer. (1994). Thoughts on technology and early childhood education. In *Young children: Active learners in a technological age,* edited by J.L. Wright and D.D. Shade. Washington, D.C.: National Association for the Education of Young Children.

Cochran, B. (1998). Unpublished interview.

Hakansson, J. (1998). Unpublished interview.

Morton, J.G. (1998). *Kids on the 'Net: Conducting Internet research in K–5 classrooms.* Portsmouth, N.H.: Heinemann.

Morton, J.G. (1996). Birds of a Feather, Mendocino Unified School District. http://www.mcn.org/ed/cur/liv/ind/birds/

7

Videoconferencing

I believe that the school must represent present life—life as real and vital to the child as that which he carries on in the home, in the neighborhood, or on the playground.

John Dewey, 1897

For K-12 education, videoconferencing is the tool of the near future that is already being used in a small number of schools. In industry, government, and higher education, distance learning through videoconferencing has proven to be a successful and cost-effective means of communication. Videoconferencing adds live two-way video to a phone conversation; both parties see as well as hear each other.

Some school districts have already figured out that videoconferencing provides organizational benefits. These are often the reasons that school districts want to invest in videoconferencing. For example:

♦ Teachers can gather at a local site in the district and "attend" a class at a distant university.

♦ The district can offer professional development opportunities and save travel costs.

♦ Meetings that would otherwise require time-consuming and expensive travel can sometimes be replaced with videoconferences.

♦ A teacher with unusual expertise on a topic can share that expertise with classes in other schools.

♦ At the high school level, the difficulty of finding teachers for some advanced courses can be solved by offering the class simultaneously at more than one school via videoconferencing.

♦ Advanced high school students can take a course at a university without leaving their high school.

Videoconferencing can have wonderful classroom uses in elementary schools as well. For example, it has been found to be highly effective in teaching music to preschool children (Gouzouasis 1994). It also allows children to go places where they could not otherwise go and meet people they could not otherwise meet. In the past, schools relied on movies, videotapes, and occasional field trips to give children these experiences; videoconferencing can now bring the world into the classroom in very real ways. It has the potential to be highly interactive, which is exactly

> *Videoconferencing allows children to go places where they could not otherwise go and meet people they could not otherwise meet.*

the characteristic that makes it appropriate for young children. Just like movies, videotapes, and field trips, videoconferencing should be closely connected to instruction—it should not be just an interesting add-on.

Let's return to the hypothetical situation described at the beginning of Chapter 1:

> You have organized much of the social studies and science curriculum for the year around the theme, *Community Connections*. With your help, the class poses two major questions:
>
> ◆ How do the people who work in our community help each other?
>
> ◆ How is our community connected to the natural setting where we live?
>
> To address the first question, children brainstorm a list of people's needs and a list of jobs that help people fill these needs. They pick certain jobs about which they want to know more. From their interests, you plan walking field trips within the community that allow you to tie mapping skills to the unit. Throughout these trips you take photos, which your students use to recall and sequence events, process their ideas, and draw and write about what they have learned. In several cases, children have asked follow-up questions by e-mail, and been delighted by the quick and thoughtful responses.
>
> In the course of this unit, you find that many children have fears about the local hospital, a place that is strictly off-limits to visit. None of the children can remember ever being inside the hospital, but they associate it with their experiences with sickness and death in their families. This hospital, like many others, has videoconferencing equipment. The hospital's community outreach staff helps you set up a videoconference with a nurse in the pediatrics ward, who takes the children on a tour. An unexpected bonus is that the nurse happens to know one of the children in your class. She agrees to answer further questions by e-mail, and the children agree to send their artwork to be displayed in the halls of the pediatric unit.

Videoconferencing Options

High-quality videoconferencing requires special phone lines, such as ISDN or T1, which are available from local phone companies. In addition to the cost of installation and service, the long-distance charges are several times higher than equivalent voice phone calls.

Videoconferencing also requires special videoconferencing equipment. Desktop units that connect to personal computers are a reasonably priced option, but they limit the number of students who can be seen from the distant site, or who can see the monitor at one time. Larger videoconferencing units are available that require a more substantial investment by the school.

More information about videoconferencing can be found on the Pacific Bell Knowledge Network Explorer Web site (http://www.kn.pacbel.com).

CU-See Me, a program developed at Cornell University that is free to educators, makes videoconferencing over the Internet possible with an inexpensive video input device, a computer, and Internet access. This option is very low cost, but it is also low quality; the image is very slow and jerky. Some teachers report that the lag time for the image is too distracting for young students, while others claim that the students get used to it, and the lag time stops being an issue. *CU-See Me* is the only option currently available to a classroom teacher without the school's commitment to videoconferencing. The downside, in addition to the quality issue, is that it takes some technical skills to set up. Without a commitment from the school, teachers have to deal with the technical issues themselves. More information on *CU-See Me* can be found on the Global Schoolhouse Web site (http://www.gsn.org).

High quality, lower cost videoconferencing will be a practical option in the future. School district networks that use high-speed lines will be able to videoconference over the Internet, which will eliminate long-distance phone charges.

Videoconferencing at the Education First Demonstration Sites

The Pacific Bell Education First Demonstration Sites had the opportunity to spend three years experimenting with videoconferencing to learn how to make it meaningful for students of all ages. They had support from Pacific Bell to find videoconferencing partners and resolve the technical issues. They also had support on the instructional end from Education for the Future and from three research fellows at San Diego State University. The support the schools gave each other was also extremely important. Collaboration between teachers at the sites, using videoconferencing and e-mail, improved instructional strategies across the board, as teachers learned from each other.

Use of the technology fell into some broad categories:

- Classes used videoconferencing, as a complement to e-mail and other Internet uses, for specific purposes such as meeting E-mail Buddies.

- Teachers developed instructional units tied to the curriculum because of an existing opportunity to participate in a worthwhile videoconference.

- Two or more classes at different schools built ongoing relationships, often centered around a common theme or area of study. In the process, teachers also used videoconferencing for their own professional development.

- Classes took virtual field trips, usually as the culminating experiences of instructional units.

Because videoconferencing was so new, and the uses that I witnessed were confined to these three schools, I have included the best examples from grades K–5 as long as they can reasonably be modified for young children.

Videoconferencing as a Complement to E-mail

E-mail and videoconferencing are both excellent complementary ways to communicate. It's much easier to develop a relationship, including E-mail Buddies or Key Pals, once people have met each other. When meeting in person isn't possible due to distance, videoconferencing provides an experience that is very close to being in the same room.

Two kindergarten classes developed an ongoing relationship by e-mail, sending daily messages back and forth that told about the highlights of the day. The purposes of the exchange were to have an authentic, engaging reason for the teachers to model the writing process with their classes and, at the same time, give children time to assess their day's work.

Prior to beginning the e-mail exchange, the classes met by videoconference. Children took turns introducing themselves, and then each group sang a song to the other that had been rehearsed. Periodically, the classes reconnect by videoconference, which makes their contacts by e-mail more meaningful.

Teacher-Developed Units That Build on Videoconferencing Opportunities

The books of children's author Eve Bunting have always been favorites at Juarez Lincoln Accelerated School. When the third and fourth grade teachers learned that the Pasadena Public Library would soon host a videoconference with this author, teachers jumped at the possibility to build a unit around her work. For the month preceding the videoconference, students read many of the author's books and teachers read them aloud in class. Students made posters, created book jackets, and wrote book reports. They examined the questions and answers on Eve Bunting's Web site so that they would create questions for the videoconference that were not already answered.

The teachers initially assumed that the videoconference would be the highlight for the children, but quickly found that the videoconference motivated the children throughout the unit.

The videoconference created an authentic reason for children to practice presentation skills. They were concerned about how their class would look and what the distant classes and the author would think of them. They practiced videoconferencing ahead of time and reviewed the videotape of their practice sessions. An unplanned but welcome outcome of the unit was improved oral presentation skills. The full unit appears as an example at the end of this chapter.

> *I felt like I was talking to a real person! When can we do this again?*
>
> *Third grade student*

Ongoing Relationships Between Classes

The value of ongoing relationships between classes turned out to be deeper and greater than anyone expected. It was especially meaningful when two classes from schools with significantly different ethnic and socioeconomic compositions developed ongoing relationships. Appreciation of diversity is a fundamental aspect of the social studies curriculum, yet one that is hard to achieve without direct contact between children of different cultures. Videoconferencing in conjunction with e-mail allows children to know children they could not otherwise know, thereby learning about the cultures of their distant friends.

Figure 7.1. Students in Two Classes Develop an Ongoing Relationship

Nothing could demonstrate this more clearly than Deena Zarlin's account of the relationship that developed between her class in Mendocino, a small rural town on the northern California coast, and Lupe Guerrera's class at Bryant Elementary school in the Mission District of San Francisco.

Lessons from a Spanish Lesson

It was a Friday in May at 9:30 a.m. Three advanced high school Spanish students, Wheylan, Laura and Scott, arrived in my fifth grade class to teach their weekly Spanish lesson. This time, though, something was a bit different. Wheylan was carrying a pile of clothing and started the session by slipping a very full, colorful skirt over his jeans. He immediately had the group's attention. Scott recorded the Spanish words on the white board while Laura taught pronunciation. Before long Wheylan was covered in blouse, vest, hats and scarves. The class was joyfully calling out "falda, blusa, sombrero." It was quite a sight.

Whenever interesting things are happening in the classroom, I immediately want to draw a colleague in to share the pleasure of watching powerful learning take place. Of course everyone in a school is busy. It's rare to find the live body who is free to catch the moment in progress. This time I knew just what to do with that sharing impulse. I would call in my colleague, Lupe Guerrero. No matter that Lupe was in another school 150 miles away. We both had desktop videoconferencing units in our classrooms.

In August 1995 I began working with Virginia Davis, Bryant Elementary's technology coordinator, as part of the Ghostwriter project. Lupe and I had been working together since January 1996. He teaches a Spanish bilingual 4–5 grade class at Bryant in San Francisco. Since January our students had been key-pals, sending e-mail regularly. Videoconferences between pairs or small groups went on four days a week. Lupe's students helped us to write letters in Spanish to our Nicaraguan pen pals and a few times gave us practice with pronunciation. We shared a Women's History Month program with them; they shared a Cinco de Mayo program with us. A 5th grade trip to San Francisco, with a visit to our pals at Bryant, was in the works.

Lupe, Virginia and I had established a strong collegial relationship through hours of communication via e-mail, videoconferencing and a few face-to-face meetings at conferences and workshops. It's not unusual for my class to receive calls from Virginia to showcase the videoconferencing technology when special visitors come through Bryant. We do the same when visitors come to Mendocino. We're all used to a level of spontaneity.

There is always a student in Lupe's classroom whose job it is to answer incoming video calls. I thought that student might enjoy seeing how we learn Spanish so decided to call in. When Lupe's student answered, I told him to let Mr. Guerrero know that we had a Spanish lesson in progress and that a few of his students might want to see how we are learning the language. Lupe's message was, "Call us back on the Eclipse." Bryant has a larger VC unit in the tech center, run by Virginia, just outside Lupe's classroom. We placed the call again and found that instead of just a few students, Lupe had dropped what he was doing and brought his whole class into the lab to participate. Though I hadn't intended to interrupt his schedule, he decided to grab, on faith, what seemed like a teachable moment. Indeed it turned out to be so.

Soon students from Bryant were standing up identifying their clothing in Spanish. By now the high school students were completely enthralled with the technology. They began conducting the class for students in both schools (receiving corrections of their pronunciation from the Bryant kids as the class progressed!) A game of Simon Says ensued with students in Mendocino and San Francisco turning in circles (de la vuelta), singing (canten) and touching their hair (tocense el pelo) when Simón dicío.

What was going on here? We know that Mendocino students benefited from instruction by Bryant's native Spanish speakers and Bryant students took pride in having a valuable skill to offer peers and older students, but also:

1. Traditional classroom isolation was overcome. The walls had collapsed. Space and time were not limiting factors.

2. Students across cultural, geographical and age boundaries were connected to one another with a common learning purpose. Our diversity was an asset.

3. Trust, developed through communications enabled by technology, allowed a new learning community to be formed.

4. Technology was used to strengthen human relationships.

5. School became a place where real things happen in a spontaneous and joyful way.

6. Memorable learning took place for all.

Deena Zarlin (1996)

Videoconferencing, Collaboration, and Professional Development

When a substantial relationship exists between two classes, as did in the example above, it ends up being as deep a learning opportunity for teachers as for students. During their extended period of collaboration, Deena Zarlin and Lupe Guerrero began leaving the videoconferencing technology on all day, once a week. (The demonstration site grants included long-distance phone charges.) The interactions that occurred as a result were similar to what happens when two colleagues who respect each other's teaching have adjacent classrooms with a doorway between them. The students and the teachers benefited from the informal collaboration, as well as from the more formal projects planned in common.

I have often wondered what would happen if more teachers could have videoconferencing partners within their schools or districts. How much easier it would be to learn from each other without the need to leave the class with a substitute teacher. Videoconferencing provides the potential for peer collaboration and coaching that would be very difficult to attain through traditional means.

Virtual Field Trips

If children's understanding of the world is built on concrete experience, as child development theorists tell us, then providing rich experiences outside the classroom, as well as inside it, give children building blocks with which to develop concepts about how the world works. It is for this reason that teachers value field trips. These trips also provide the raw materials for writing, because children write best from experience.

Virtual field trips make it possible for children to travel beyond the walls of their classroom without actually leaving the room. Although a real field trip may still be the best option, it is often not a possibility, as in the case described below, also from Juarez-Lincoln School.

> Bob Birdsell and Kristina Shoopack's fifth and sixth grade classes were studying marine life with help by e-mail from biologists at the Monterey Bay Aquarium. Although the aquarium is hundreds of miles from the school, students knew that they would be able to take a virtual field trip at the end of the unit. Working in groups, students researched the marine animals of their choice. They used a variety of research sources: books and magazines, CD-ROMs, the Web, and e-mail. When they couldn't find answers to questions, they e-mailed the questions to the scientists at the aquarium.

> On the day of the field trip, their guide took them on the same tour they would have experienced if they had been there in person, by using portable videoconferencing equipment for that purpose. Children could stop along the way, ask questions, and even ask the guide to focus in closer on a point of interest.

> As told to the author

Videoconferencing Practices in K–3 Classrooms

Virtual Field Trips Designed for Young Children

Interview participants emphasized certain criteria that are important for young children who take virtual field trips. These are similar to guidelines for field trips involving young children in general, but also take into account the fact that virtual field trips are a step removed from the actual experience.

Special criteria for virtual field trips are:

♦ *In most cases, virtual field trips should visit places or people that are already familiar.* For example, visiting children at another school by videoconference is going to a familiar place, even if the children have not visited that particular school before. For very young children, virtual field trips to parents' workplaces are a way to allay children's anxiety about separation and to provide information about the world of work. These field trips will become more possible as videoconferencing becomes more commonplace.

♦ *In certain cases, virtual field trips are a good way to learn about new things that may be frightening in person.* Barbara Scales, of the University of California Child Study Center, sees virtual field trips as a good way to introduce preschoolers to the kindergarten they will attend. Taking a virtual field trip has a degree of safety that makes it ideal for introducing certain experiences (1997). The virtual hospital visit, mentioned earlier, fits this category well.

♦ *Return visits are ideally suited to the needs of young children, and to the use of videoconferencing.* To maximize learning, young children would ideally visit the same place more than once in the course of a unit to get answers to questions that arise from the first visit.

Connecting Real Events, Videoconferencing, and Writing

Repeating experiences with some variation is important to children as they construct an understanding of the world around them. Children often seek repetition, as if they instinctively know that they need the same or similar experiences many times to create meaning from them. Discussing, documenting, and writing help children in this process. A potential use of videoconferencing posed by Barbara Scales illustrates this point.

Imagine this:

A talented storyteller is scheduled monthly at the library in a nearby town. The storyteller uses various props as she tells and acts out the story. A kindergarten class attends the first session in October, and the experience sets off a fascination with storytelling by the children. The teacher would like to bring the students back every month, but cannot provide the transportation. Instead, the class is able to walk a few blocks to the local community college where videoconferencing is already available, and be part of the virtual audience several times during the school year.

After the initial visit in person, children could:

♦ Discuss what they have seen.

♦ Write, using the pictures they have taken for sequencing and organizing.

♦ Pose questions as they reflect on their experience.

♦ Revisit by videoconference to find answers to their own questions and to hear a second story.

♦ Review their original written work.

♦ Write again, or revise.

Videoconferencing and Self-Reflection

One unexpected benefit of videoconferencing at the Education First Demonstration Sites was the degree to which students were able to reflect on their presentation skills and the quality of their work (Bernhardt 1998). Although this was most obvious in older children, it was true even at the second and third grade levels. Typical comments from students were: "Did you see those children smile when I told my story?" or "They didn't seem to understand what I said. I'm going to practice more next time."

These and similar comments, heard by teachers over and over again, suggest that videoconferencing allows children to see themselves from the audience's point of view. In videoconferencing, each party can see the other and see themselves at the same time. Both images can be displayed simultaneously. Children therefore are able to watch themselves from the perspective of the audience.

The videoconference can also be recorded on a regular videocassette, allowing the class to review it again. With young children, reviewing the tape is important in the reflection process. Hakansson (1998) explains:

> If children are actively engaged in doing something, their focus is on that moment. They don't have the perspective to observe themselves while they are engaged in the activity. It's when they are finished that they can reflect, if they have photos or video that allow them to become part of the audience. These images make it possible for the child to step outside their own perspective to assess their work. Now, it is not just the child's work; the child becomes part of the audience and sees the work on the screen or sees the pictures. If the child is not pleased with what he sees, he will do it differently next time. By the time children are five or six years old, they

start developing the social consciousness to want to meet the expectation of their peers.

Self-reflection is a process that is very difficult for young children, but very necessary for improving the quality of work. Videoconferencing and videotaping are excellent tools to help children develop this self-awareness.

An Example Unit That Integrates Videoconferencing

The unit that follows was developed at Juarez-Lincoln Accelerated School in San Diego, California, by teachers Sharon Quinn, Rebecca Feder, Linda Hutchison, Teresita Modelo, and Kristina Shoopack.

Meet the Author

Grade Level: 3 to 4 (applicable to any grade)

Subject: Language Arts

When the opportunity arose for our students to videoconference with children's author Eve Bunting, we recognized the potential of using the videoconference as the finale in an instructional unit that would motivate students to read many of the fine stories by this author and to write about them. We designed a unit in which students read a variety of genres, learned about the writing process from the author's point of view, and experienced writing as something that "real" people do in their work. Although we thought that the videoconference would be the high point, the entire unit turned out to be a much richer experience for students than we ever imagined.

Student Expectations

- ♦ Students will demonstrate ability to develop questions that elicit information not available from other resources.
- ♦ Students will demonstrate insight by responding artistically and in written form to literature.
- ♦ Students will recognize and appreciate the writing process used by a published author.

(This unit was developed prior to the existence of California State Standards. However, the expectations could easily be aligned with state standards anywhere.)

Unit Preparation

We gathered a wide variety of books by the author, Eve Bunting. We coordinated with the San Diego County Office of Education to plan a process for asking questions because several schools would be involved in the videoconference. All questions were submitted to the author ahead of time so that she could address many of them in her presentation.

Students needed a variety of skills and knowledge to be successful:

- They needed to practice asking and writing questions so that they would be prepared to ask quality questions.
- They needed to be familiar with the author's books.
- They needed practice in videoconferencing, so that they would know how to project a good image of themselves and the school.

Student artwork was posted on bulletin boards so that it would be visible during the conference.

Details of the Unit

For the month preceding the conference, students read many of the author's books, and teachers read them aloud in class. Student choice of books was an important motivator. Students made posters, created book jackets, and wrote book reports.

Students examined the questions and answers on Eve Bunting's Web site, so that they would create questions for the videoconference that were not already answered.

Use of Technology

- Students used the Internet to examine the author's Web site.
- Teachers used e-mail to coordinate between sites.
- Videoconferencing was used to meet the author, who was located at the public library in Pasadena, California.

Assessment

Student responses to the elements of a story were assessed through:

- Classroom discussion
- Artwork

♦ Written work (poetry, journals, reports)

Additionally, students were assessed using:

- ♦ Teacher observation during the teleconference.
- ♦ Student interest in checking out the author's books.
- ♦ Thank-you letters to the author and letters to parents that reflected upon the experience.

Modifications to Ensure That All Students Learn

Partner reading was used to help students comprehend and decode what they read. The author's books have such a range of reading levels that this unit is appropriate for all students.

Unanticipated Outcomes

- ♦ Some of the students with learning disabilities were able to participate at a very high level because the unit used strategies that are verbal, visual, and auditory. In many cases, the quality of their questions were excellent.
- ♦ Student presentation skills improved.
- ♦ Students were able to identify redundant questions—questions that had already been addressed by the author.
- ♦ The entire unit was so motivating that the videoconference was just one piece of it, from the point of view of the students.
- ♦ The videoconference motivated many students to go to the public library in our area.

For More Information

Visit the Juarez-Lincoln Web site:

http://www.cvesd.k12.ca.us/jl

Summary

Videoconferencing can make it possible for children to travel beyond the confines of their classroom and to have the experiences that stimulate conceptual development and writing skills.

Some of the best uses include:

- ♦ Collaboration with other classes over time that allows children of different cultures to know each other.

- ◆ Visits to familiar places such as zoos, or to places that might be frightening in person but are safe from a distance.

- ◆ Talks with favorite authors and other adults who are experts in an area of interest to the children.

Videoconferencing allows children to see themselves from the point of view of the audience, motivating them to work on their presentation skills. In addition, there are endless possibilities for teachers to improve teaching strategies through collaboration.

References

Bernhardt, V.L. (1998). Education First demonstrates success with technology. *ASCD Curriculum/Technology Quarterly* (Winter), 8 (2), 5–6.

Dewey, J. (1951 [1897]). My pedagogic creed. In *Dewey on education: Selections with an introduction and notes by Martin S. Dworkin*. New York: Bureau of Publications, Teachers College, 1951.

The Global Schoolhouse. (1998). http://www.gsn.org

Gouzouasis, P. (1994). Video conferencing with preschool children: Mass communications media in music instruction. In *Educational Multimedia and Hyper Media*, Proceedings of ED-MEDIA 94, World Conference on Educational Multimedia and Hypermedia. Vancouver, British Columbia, June 25–30, 1994.

Hakansson, J. (1998). Unpublished interview.

Pacific Bell Knowledge Network Explorer. (1998). http://www.kn.pacbel.com

Quinn, S., R. Feder, L. Hutchison, T. Modelo, and K. Shoopack. (1997). Meet the Author, Juarez-Lincoln Accelerated School. http://www.cvesd.k12.ca.us/jl

Scales, B. (1997). Unpublished interview.

Zarlin, D. (1996). Mission-Mendo Exchange, Mendocino Unified School District. http://www.mms.mendocino.k12.ca.us/gs/ca/dz/Men-Mis.html

8

Getting Started and Finding Help

It takes more than an attitude and a costume to do this job.

Attributed to Batman

Computers and other technology tools have become far more accessible to teachers and students in the past few years. In its annual Technology in Education report in 1998, Market Data Retrieval (MDR) found that 85 percent of schools and 44 percent of classrooms now have Internet access. These figures are more than double those of two years earlier. For a long time, lack of access was a primary impediment to the integration of technology into the curriculum. As access continues to improve, the primary issue becomes one of professional development; teachers need to learn how to integrate technology in meaningful ways and they must acquire the technical skills to do so.

In some schools, a trailblazer has led the way in using technology in the classroom, providing both a model and support for other teachers. If that person is especially effective, the school is likely to create a schoolwide vision for technology use, create a plan to get there, and figure out how to free that person as a technology coordinator, at least part-time.

Without this level of support, implementing the use of technology tools in the classroom can seem overwhelming, even if you are clear about how you want to use technology with young children. The purposes of this chapter are to provide some guidance for individuals who want to get started and to identify additional sources of help.

Although you alone can do quite a bit as you implement your personal vision of how to integrate technology in your classroom, ultimately technology will have a far greater impact on children's learning when the entire school pursues a common vision. Chapter 9 addresses moving from a personal vision to a schoolwide vision that affects all students.

Creating a Supportive Environment

The Computer Center

The computer center should be set up in a spot where young children can easily use it in their work, and adults can easily supervise and assist. Although many decisions about computer placement are controlled by the location of electrical outlets, it is important to place them so that the teacher can see the students work at all times.

Figure 8.1. Put the Computer Center in a Spot Where You Can Easily Assist Students

This allows teachers to:

◆ Monitor progress.

◆ Be aware if students need help.

◆ Know if the Internet is being used.

Teachers sometimes think that the screen will be too distracting to other students who are working in the room. According to Haugland and Wright, "There is no need to enclose the computer area. Children are not distracted by other activities and in fact much learning goes on as peers pass by and watch and talk about what is happening" (1997). In an interactive classroom in which children are accustomed to more than one activity occurring at a time, the computer soon stops being a novelty and becomes a learning tool for all to use.

By following a few basic principles in setting up the computer center, you can protect both the students and the equipment:

◆ Secure electrical cords or cables out of reach.

◆ Use a surge protector to guard against electrical damage to the computer.

◆ Place the monitor to avoid glare on the screen from outside windows.

◆ Place the computer center near other centers where children work in small groups, such as near math manipulatives, a library center, or writing center.

- Place the computer on a table or desk that is low enough for children to sit comfortably in a chair and have the keyboard at waist level and the monitor at eye level.

- Use a table that is large enough to accommodate the computer and printer and still have work space for children to use for materials related to their work.

- Provide at least two chairs for each computer, and allow space for children to bring additional chairs as needed.

- Avoid positioning a computer near or under a chalkboard; chalk dust can cause damage.

- Avoid areas that are near water or food sources to minimize the possibility of hardware damage due to spills.

Classroom Management Issues

Managing access to the computer can seem like a daunting task, especially if there is only one computer in the class. It requires careful management for students to have equal access to the computer for collaborating in writing or other projects. Classroom management techniques for this purpose are similar to those used for other learning centers:

- Assigning partners or groups.
- Scheduling time slots.
- Creating a rotational system for learning centers.
- Creating a system that allows children to know when their turn will come.
- Tracking student participation.

All these help ensure that all students have access to the computer to create their work and to learn computer skills, regardless of their persistence in getting a turn. In classrooms in which children are used to working in learning centers, they are active participants in the management system. Children learn to help through such processes as:

- Placing their name cards in a pocket chart to wait for a turn.
- Checking off their names when they have finished their turn.
- Taking turns at the keyboard when working with a partner.

- ◆ Following expectations in caring for equipment.
- ◆ Calling the next group.

In addition to these basic management structures that apply to learning centers in general, a few are specific to computers. The following list of ideas may be helpful in managing computers in the classroom:

- ◆ *Keep the computer on and available all day.* When the computer is used as a tool that helps children develop academic skills, using it is an appropriate activity almost any time. Many more students will get a chance to use the computer if it is available throughout the day.

- ◆ *Ask volunteers to help type first drafts.* In the ideal world, there would be enough computers in classrooms for students to use them to compose first drafts. If computer access makes this impossible, try to recruit a parent volunteer to enter first drafts of student writing on the computer, exactly as written. When the students have time to use the computer, they can concentrate on revising and editing their work, rather than on entering it.

- ◆ *Recruit older students or parents when you begin new projects.* Volunteers can help students become competent more quickly when they are learning to use new software or new techniques. The purpose is to move students as quickly as possible to focus on the content of their work, rather than on the software.

- ◆ *Use the "each-one-teach-one" approach.* Teach the first two students a task such as copying and pasting a photo from a file on the hard drive into a word-processed document. These students then each teach two others. The process continues until all students have been taught and have taught someone else.

- ◆ *Occasionally, give students a full day to work uninterrupted.* For large projects, especially at the second and third grade level, consider allowing partners or groups to have a "computer day"—one day when they work exclusively on their project for an extended period of time. This strategy works well when students are preparing a major project using the computer.

- ◆ *Keep young children's work on the hard drive or an external drive.* Don't expect young children to manage their work on floppy disks, which are easily lost or damaged.

♦ *Use a utility that provides file security. Children are instinctive experimenters.* They love to see what happens if they put folders in the trash and create new ones! Give children access only to the files they need, by using programs such as *At Ease* or *Fool Proof.*

♦ *Monitor CD-ROMs closely.* Some software programs now require CD-ROMs to work. These should be monitored carefully, allowing only those in current use to be available to students. They are easily misplaced in a busy classroom.

♦ *Have a computer helper.* There are many ways students can help: turning the computer on and off each day; making sure all the CD-ROMs are put away at the end of the day; and checking for e-mail.

Helping Students Understand Their Part in Large Projects

Developing a large class project such as a class multimedia project requires careful pre-planning. Without support, children may not be able to understand their role in the success of the whole project and how others may be dependent on their work. Brainstorming, mapping techniques, and developing class agreements all help students understand the global picture and their personal role in making the project successful.

A large bulletin board that displays a diagram of the project, with students' names marking their part of the work, helps children gain an understanding of where they fit into the larger plan. This is especially important in projects that use hypertext or buttons for navigating (multimedia), because the navigational process itself is invisible.

Equity Issues

Teachers must be diligent about issues of gender and ethnicity as they relate to computer use. Monitoring and tracking computer time is just the beginning to approaching the issues of equity. Whether or not an activity is computer-based, biases toward one learning style affects student success and may equate to cultural biases (Chisholm 1995). Probably the most important way to ensure equity is to structure computer activities so that they appeal to different groups of children equally and can be accomplished by students of varying learning styles.

For example, competitiveness between individuals is considered a negative quality in some cultures. Many computer simulations of "real" problems intentionally set up competitive situations as a way to motivate students. Teachers' knowledge about cultural and gender differences can make the difference in children's ability and desire to use the technology to support learning.

Figure 8.2. For Many Students, Collaboration is a Key Element in Learning

In a study of the ability of nine-to-twelve-year-old students to solve computer-generated science puzzles, pairs of students who shared a computer were able to solve many more problems than pairs who worked together but on parallel computers, or students who worked alone. Boys who worked alone did considerably better than girls who worked alone, but there was no significant difference in the problem-solving ability of pairs of girls compared to pairs of boys (Inkpen, Booth, Klawe, and Upitis 1995). Although this study involves older students, it points out that the cooperative aspects of learning are more crucial to some groups of students than to others. Equity means recognizing that gender and culture affect children's learning styles and preferences; these differences should be a primary consideration in designing projects.

The good news is that researchers who study gender equity have found no significant difference in attitude toward computers between boys and girls in the early primary grades (Snider and Badgett 1995; Knezek and Miyashita 1993; Beeson and Williams 1985; Lipinski 1984). Differences did not appear until after the third grade (Knezek and Miyashita 1993). Girls who used computers in their classrooms in the early grades tended to have more positive attitudes in follow-up surveys than those who did not, leading some to speculate that early computer use may help prevent gender differences from developing.

> *Girls who used computers in their classrooms in the early grades tended to have more positive attitudes in follow-up surveys than those who did not, leading some to speculate that early computer use may help prevent gender differences from developing.*

Finding Help

If you aren't experienced in using technology tools yourself, you will probably want to take a few classes offered specifically for teachers. These classes generally combine technical information with discussions about using technology in the classroom. From there, consider joining one of the professional organizations that supports educational use of technology, subscribing to journals, and using on-line resources. Don't forget about tapping into community resources; there are many people who are pleased to be able to share their knowledge if they can see that it makes a difference in the lives of children.

Professional Organizations and Journals

The *National Educational Computing Association (NECA)* is an organization of professional organizations. Its Web site describes member organizations and has links to them, which makes them easy to find. Many of the member organizations have worthwhile journals or newsletters. Start with the NECA site (http://www.neccsite.org/html/neca_cooperating_societies.html).

Instructional Resources on the Web

Any discussion of Web resources for education must begin with the *Educational Resources Information Center (ERIC)*, developed by the U.S. government's National Library of Education (http://ericir.syr.edu/Eric). This is far more than a site to help educators integrate technology; it contains a searchable database of over 950,000 abstracts of books or journal articles written about educational practice and research since the late 1960s. You can find almost anything about education using ERIC, including information about using technology.

Figure 8.3. The Educational Resource Information Center (ERIC) Searchable Database

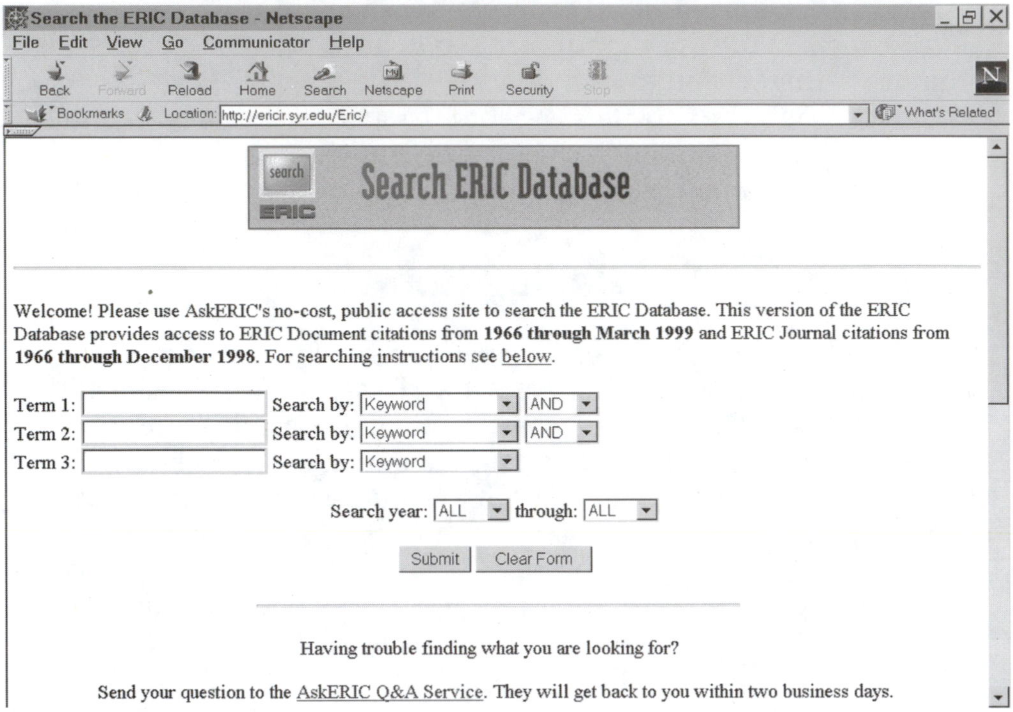

There are so many other Web sites that support teachers' efforts to integrate technology tools into the curriculum that any specific list is bound to omit many useful resources. Therefore, the approach taken here is to examine the types of sources and give an example of one excellent Web site within each category. From these few sources, you will be able to find so many others that you will soon develop your own favorite list.

The sources of help fall into several categories:

- ◆ State departments of education
- ◆ University education departments
- ◆ School districts and county offices
- ◆ Nonprofit educational organizations
- ◆ Corporations with educational support programs
- ◆ Commercial sites designed for education

♦ Individual schools and teachers

♦ Newsgroups and listservs

The examples you will find in the discussion of these categories should provide you with starting points to find the information you need, whether you are looking for technology-infused projects, space to house your Web site, or research links for information about a topic. All of the sites below include links to other teacher resources.

However, a word of warning is in order. Web addresses tend to change rapidly, and although these examples have been stable for some time, they too may change. If you can't find them with the URL (Uniform Resource Locator or Web address) provided, try searching by name using a search engine such as *Yahoo* or *Alta Vista*.

State Departments of Education

In addition to all the other information found on state department of education Web sites, there is often a section to help teachers to use resources on the Web. Research links to other Web sites are often organized to relate to state standards and curriculum. Many states provide instructional units and on-line projects as well.

One that I especially like at the K–3 level is *Cyberguides,* part of the *Schools of California Online Resources for Education (SCORE)* language arts site (http://www.sdcoe.k12.ca.us/score/cyberguide.html). It provides an excellent source of units appropriate for grades K–3 based on high-quality children's literature that include research links to other Internet sites. All units on this site are designed by teachers and are tied to the California Language Arts Standards. For example, in a unit about the book *Frog and Toad Are Friends,* by Arnold Lobel, Linda Scott provides links to child-friendly Internet sites about frogs and toads and suggestions for specific activities.

Universities

Some universities, especially those that have instructional technology programs, host sites specifically for educators that include research links by topic. A few universities sponsor project-based interactive units that use the Internet for communication, although these are usually intended for older students.

Instructional Technologies Connections (http://www.cudenver. edu/~mryder/itcon.html), at the University of Colorado at Denver, provides a simply organized, easy-to-use hotlist (hypertext list) of excellent resources, including many that are valuable in the primary grades.

School Districts and County Offices

Many school districts and county departments of education, especially large ones, have Web sites that support teachers who use the Internet. One of the most comprehensive I have seen is *Teams Distance Learning*, part of the Los Angeles County Office of Education Web site (http://teams.lacoe.edu/). You don't have to be from a Los Angeles county school to take advantage of the many projects and resources offered. *Teams* has many resources that support using the Internet with young children.

Nonprofit Educational Organizations

Many nonprofit organizations support teachers in using Internet-infused units, but perhaps none is as well known, and deservedly so, as the *Global Schoolnet Foundation* and its Web site, the *Global Schoolhouse* (http://www.gsh.org). The site provides a forum for children, teachers, and parents to share their work. In addition to the projects they sponsor, there is an Internet Project Registry where teachers can post or find interactive units appropriate to their grade level and the interests of their students. The Internet unit at the end of Chapter 5 was posted on the Project Registry. The *Global Schoolnet Foundation* also provides technical information about a variety of issues (including low-cost video-conferencing) and space on its server for schools to publish student work.

Corporations with Educational
Support Programs

Many corporations have Web sites designed specifically to support education that are loaded with excellent references and useful information. *Blue Web'n* (http://www.kn.pacbell.com/wired/bluewebn/index.html), part of Pacific Bell's *Knowledge Network Explorer,* provides one of the best searchable databases for collaborative projects and other resources. The quality of projects is consistently exceptional, although there are only a few projects listed in the database for young children. A hotlist of other sites' hotlists, searchable by subject, is one of the many other valuable options.

Figure 8.4. The Global Schoolhouse Web Site

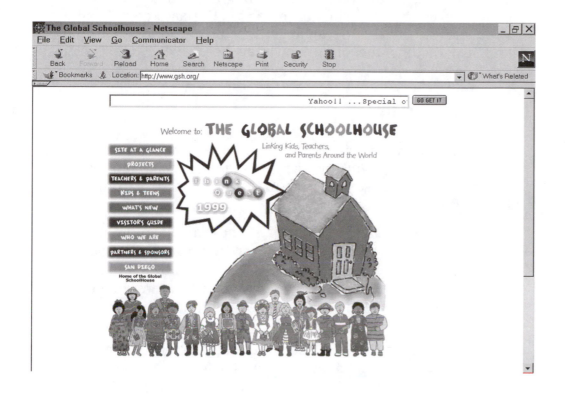

Commercial Sites Designed for Education

There are very helpful commercial sites that require paid subscriptions, but they generally provide at least some free access, either to certain areas of the site or by offering a free trial period. *Classroom Connect* (http://www.classroomconnect.com) has one such site that allows nonsubscribers into many of the teacher resources. Their resources are excellent, but they do reserve the best for paid subscribers. Some other commercial sites are free but are supported by advertising.

Individual Schools and Teachers

Some individual schools have developed Web sites that rival the best professional sites in providing Web-based resources for teachers. Such is the case with *Vose Elementary School* in Beaverton, Oregon (http://www.beavton.k12.or.us/vose/index.html). Because this is an elementary school, care has been taken to provide K–3 resources as well as upper grades resources. This site also has examples of student work.

Newsgroups and Listservs

Some newsgroups and listservs are groups of educators that support each other in using technology in the classroom. Posting a request for help is one way to get specific questions answered, and just reading the discussion may help avoid unexpected problems.

Software Help

Sometimes when I visit schools teachers seek me out with very specific questions about software programs. In fact, I am not an expert in most of these programs, but I do know where to go to get answers:

♦ *Manuals and built-in help menus.* These are the most obvious, but not always the clearest source of help. If you are using a version of the software that allows it to be run on many machines, you may not have access to the printed copy of the manual. It's sometimes hard to use the built-in help and perform the task at the same time.

♦ *Third-party manuals.* There are many excellent third-party manuals that are inexpensive and easy to use. I personally like the ones put out by *Peachpit Press* (http://www.peachpit.com), and often buy them before I try to learn a new program.

♦ *The manufacturer's Web site.* Usually, if you go to the manufacturer's Web site and e-mail a question about using the software, you will get a response within 24 hours.

♦ *The help phone line.* Some software companies have help lines. These are generally not 800 numbers, and you may have to wait, so try other approaches first.

Manufacturers have a corporate interest in seeing that you are pleased with their products. Educational software companies in particular tend to be responsive to teachers' difficulties and will answer your questions.

Hardware Help

Aside from the most obvious source of help—the computer manufacturer—there are a variety of Web sites that offer trouble-shooting help. The *California Technology Assistance Project (CTAP) Techcenter Help Desk* is a source that makes you feel as if you have a knowledgeable friend (http://www.rims.k12.ca.us/ctap/help/macintosh). Actually, it's a well-designed database that guides you to possible solutions. Figure 8.5 shows the help screen for Macintosh users. A Windows version also exists.

Figure 8.5 CTAP Techcenter Help Desk, Macintosh Help Screen

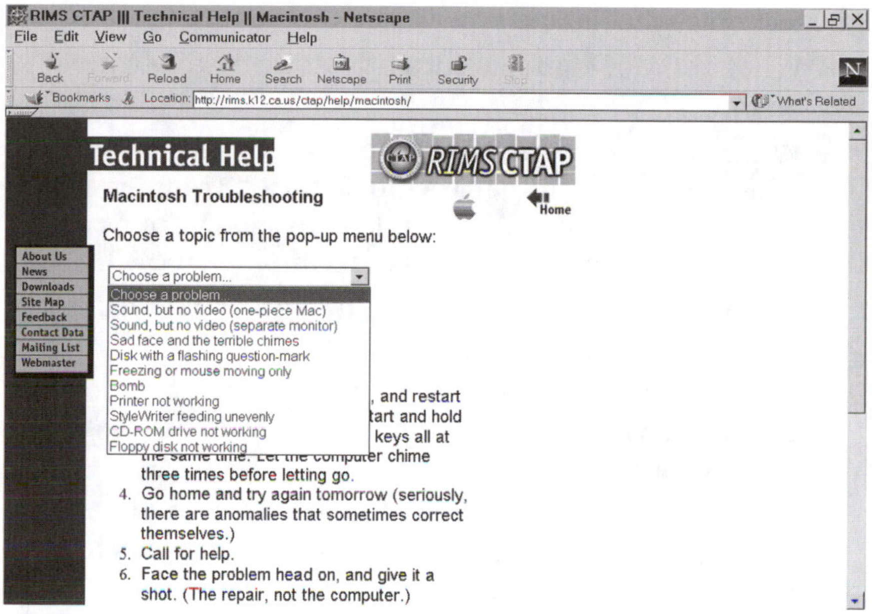

Getting Help in the Community

Parents and corporate partners are approached so often for donations that they must find it refreshing to be approached for their expertise. A note in the parent newsletter or a call to the chamber of commerce may help you find people in the community who can assist you with technical issues. Don't overlook the potential help of high school and college students.

Personal Strategic Planning

Even if you're the trailblazer and your school has not used a strategic planning approach, you can personally use this process, recognizing that change takes time, knowledge, and energy to implement. If you can answer the following questions, you will be well on your way to creating an approach to integrating technology that will work for you.

- ♦ What is your own vision for using technology tools to support the curriculum with young children?

- ♦ How does your vision align with state and district standards and benchmarks?

- ♦ Based on your vision, in five years from now, what exactly would you like your students to be doing with technology tools, and how would this affect learning?

- ♦ What are your students currently doing with technology tools?

- ♦ What would you need to implement each year to get to where you want to be? (Begin with the components that are most possible to implement given your current skill and the availability of technology tools.)

- ♦ What professional development will you need to reach your yearly goals?

- ♦ What do you currently have in the way of technology tools, and what additional technology will you need to reach your yearly goals?

- ♦ What can be funded from the school and district sources, and what will require other sources such as grants or fund-raising?

- ♦ How will you document your progress so that your track record will attract funding?

Once you are clear about your own plan and have begun to implement and document it, you may find that you have become that local expert to whom everyone else turns for support. If so, it's time to move the discussion of how technology tools can support learning to the level of the whole school.

References

Annual Technology in Education Report. (1998). Market Data Retrieval. http://www.schooldata.com

Beeson, B.S. and R.A. Williams. (1985). The effects of gender and age on preschool children's choice of the computer as a child-selected activity. *Journal of the American Society for Information Science* 36 (5): 339–41.

Blue Web'n. (1999). Pacific Bell Knowledge Network Explorer. http://www.kn.pacbell.com/wired/bluewebn/index.html

California Technology Assistance Project (CTAP). (1999). Techcenter Help Desk.
http://www.rims.k12.ca.us/ctap/help/macintosh

Chisholm, I.M. (1995/96). Computer use in a multicultural classroom. *Journal of Research on Computing in Education* 28 (Winter).

Cyberguides. (1998). Schools of California Online Resources for Education (SCORE).
http://www.sdcoe.k12.ca.us/score/cyberguide.html

Global Schoolhouse. (1998). http://www.gsh.org

Haugland, S. and J. Wright. (1997). *Young children and technology: A world of discovery.* Needham Heights, Mass.: Allyn and Bacon.

Inkpen, K., K. Booth, M. Klawe, and R. Upitis. (1995). Playing together beats playing apart, especially for girls. In *CSCL '95: Proceedings of the first international conference on computer support for collaborative learning,* edited by J.L. Schnase. and E.L. Cunnius. Mahwah, N.J.: Lawrence Erlbaum Associates.

Instructional Technologies Connections. (1998). University of Colorado at Denver.
http://www.cudenver.edu/~mryder/itcon.html

Knezek, G. and K. Miyashita. (1993). Learner dispositions related to primary school computing in three nations: 1992 results. Paper presented at the Annual Meeting of the American Educational Research Association (Atlanta, Ga., April 12–16, 1993).

Lipinski, J.M. (1984). *Competence, gender and preschoolers free play when a microcomputer is present in the classroom.* Report No. P.S. 014 454. Greensboro, N.C.: North Carolina University Family Research Center. (ERIC Document Reproduction Service No. 243 609).

National Educational Computing Association. (1998).
http://www. neccsite.org/html/neca_cooperating_societies.html

Snider, S. L. and T.L. Badgett. (1995). "I have this computer, what do I do now?" Using technology to enhance every child's learning. *Early Childhood Education Journal* 23 (2): 101–104.

Teams Distance Learning. (1999). Los Angeles County Office of Education. http://teams.lacoe.edu/

Vose School. (1998). Beaverton School District.
http://www.beavton.k12.or.us/vose/index.html

9

Taking a Schoolwide Approach

To believe that the job of a classroom teacher is to operate solely in the present with his or her charge, is to deny a school the opportunity to provide a cumulative, purposeful effect. To focus on an individual classroom and on the present resigns students to a fragmented education. If I really care about the education of "my" kids, I have to care about them before and after me; thus, I need to view what is "mine" as "ours."

Carl Glickman, 1993

In the early 1980s, when very few teachers were using computers in their classrooms, a common belief was that technology would revolutionize teaching and learning. Seymour Papert, inventor of LOGO, had recently written his now classic book, *Mindstorms: Children, Computers, and Powerful Ideas,* in which he described how computers allow children to think in ways that had not previously been possible. He predicted then that computers could change traditional educational processes. Many people hoped then that machines could do what 100 years of writing in educational psychology and philosophy had not done—bring about broad change in educational practices that would make classrooms engaging places for children to work on authentic problems. In hindsight, that expectation greatly underestimated the resiliency of institutions to resist change, as Papert recognized in his later work, *The Children's Machine: Rethinking School in the Age of the Computer* (1993).

What has changed in the two intervening decades is that there are many more teachers today than there were in 1980 who have discovered the power of technology to implement constructivist practices. These are highly creative teachers who use projects and other hands-on methods to engage children in learning and would probably do so with or without technology. Nevertheless, they have experienced the potential of technology tools to allow students to accomplish more complex and more thought-provoking work than would otherwise be possible. These teachers understand the potential link between powerful technologies and powerful learning, and can help others see this link as part of an overall school vision. If you personally felt a connection to the examples woven throughout this book, I suspect you are one of these people.

A Coherent Vision

For technology tools to truly make a difference in students' learning, schools need to step back from a focus on tools or individual classrooms and focus instead on the total educational experience that children have over many years—the basic "architecture" of the educational system. This requires coming to a consensus as a school community on very fundamental issues:

- ◆ What do we believe about how children learn that will determine our vision for the school?

- ◆ What are the fundamental things that we want students to know and be able to do?

- ◆ How much emphasis will we place on the breadth of the curriculum, as compared to giving children time to work in depth?

- ◆ What will the learning environment be like in every classroom in this school when we reach our vision?

- ◆ How can we use assessment practices to help students take control of their own learning?

Figure 9.1. Students Benefit from a Schoolwide Vision That Focuses on Developmentally Appropriate Practices

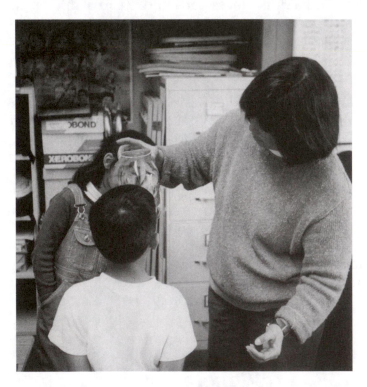

These conversations are far more difficult than discussions of technology use, but they shape what students will get from their years in school in a profound way. Technology can make a difference *schoolwide* only when:

- There is a common schoolwide vision.
- Everyone makes a commitment to implementing the vision.
- There is a detailed plan in place for implementation that includes timelines, budget, and who is responsible.
- Teachers have the ongoing professional support to make the changes in instructional practices to which they have agreed in principle.

> *For technology tools to truly make a difference in students' learning, schools need to step back from a focus on tools or individual classrooms and focus instead on the total educational experience that children have over many years—the basic "architecture" of the educational system.*

This is both an opportunity and a challenge. Unless schools address their underlying practices and assumptions about how students learn, investment in hardware and software will ultimately have very little overall impact. I have observed schools in which the technology was available, every teacher had made a commitment to use it, and teachers had been trained in the technical skills. Yet these schools had difficulty integrating technology in meaningful ways because they had no schoolwide agreements about what is meant by *excellent teaching and powerful learning.* In these schools, teachers used technology exactly as they used any other tool in the classroom—to support their existing teaching styles. Those teachers who used a hands-on, constructivist approach used technology to support their approach. Those teachers who focused more on rote learning and discrete skills used computers as electronic ditto sheets. Side by side with the wonderful uses that I have described in this book, I have seen some classrooms in which children used the Internet merely to find the answers to a list of multiple choice questions.

Implementing Technology to Achieve the Vision

At the Stanford Research Institute (SRI) Center for Technology in Learning, Barbara Means and Kerry Olson conducted nine case studies to understand more about the role of technology in supporting school reform. Their conclusion is that technology is no "silver bullet" when it comes to educational reform (Means, Olson, and Singh 1995). They found that the schools that were most successful in using technology across the curriculum, across grade levels, and in all classrooms were schools in which there was a consistently held philosophy—a schoolwide vision—about the instructional approaches to support shared instructional goals.

Those of us who worked with the Education First demonstration sites to help them implement visions that include technology observed certain conditions or strategies that moved the schools forward. These have been observed by others as well, and are consistent with Means's findings. These conditions and strategies include:

◆ A focus on the curriculum in technology planning

◆ Teacher access to technology

◆ Student access to technology in the classroom

◆ A core group of early implementers

◆ A technology coordinator who is also an instructional leader

◆ Collaboration time to work together on improving instruction

◆ Cross-age mentoring

◆ Involvement of parents and community

◆ Use of data for continuous improvement

◆ A plan for equipment maintenance

A Focus on the Curriculum in Technology Planning

Technology plans must be focused on the curriculum, rather than on equipment. Everyone needs to see and understand the purpose of integrating technology and how it will improve student learning. There must be agreement about a continuum of learning that includes technology so that children continually use and build upon the technical and academic skills and knowledge they develop from year to year. If students develop skills in using technology tools during one year and never get to practice those skills in future years, the impact is diminished.

Teacher Access to Technology

Teachers need to use technology in their own work before they can integrate it in the classroom effectively. That means that the first places that computers belong are on the desks and in the homes of teachers. Schools and districts can create a need for teachers to become technically literate by communicating with them via e-mail. Computer literacy increases further when schools or districts find the funds to provide hardware (computers, printers, etc.) to teachers in exchange for taking courses and developing instructional units. Giving teachers access to the

Internet from home allows them to find resources for students when they have the time.

Student Access to Technology in the Classroom

Access to technology, preferably in the classroom, is an obvious but not always well-planned component of integration. If computers are scarce, consider setting up movable banks of four to six computers that can be shared between several classrooms. Substantial integration into the curriculum is very difficult when computers continue to be isolated in labs, much like "the body's immune response to foreign invasion" (Papert 1993).

Figure 9.2. The Computer Is a Tool That Should Be Available to Students All Day, Just like Other Materials for Student Learning

---

A Core Group of Early Implementers

A group of trailblazers who can model and support technology integration are crucial to moving the effort schoolwide. School and district administrators are wise to recognize the role of teacher leaders and support them as they are developing technology skills; these are the people who can later provide much of the support to the rest of the staff. Schools that have a culture that includes team planning and peer coaching are more likely to succeed than schools in which teachers are expected to implement change alone. Technology is a wonderful place to begin peer mentoring and coaching in that teachers can admit that they need help in this area. For example:

> The way one school worked to integrate technology throughout their curriculum was to develop a summer institute in which teachers helped each other develop skills and instructional units. To prepare for the institute, teachers were asked how they would like to integrate technology in their classes and what they needed to learn about the technology.

> The teachers answered the questions and developed a chart showing what each wanted to learn. By the end of the month preceding the institute, much of the "wish list" was obsolete. The teachers with experience in an area had informally helped the others, once they knew what their colleagues needed. Now staff members regularly use group e-mail messages to ask for and give help.

A Technology Coordinator

Technology coordinators can play a key role if they are instructional leaders as well. Successful schools usually find a way to make the technology coordinator available to support other teachers during at least part of the teaching day. Funding may come from a combination of the school budget, grants, mentor program funds, and other sources.

Collaboration Time

In schools and districts that build collaboration time into the schedule for groups of teachers to work together to improve instructional strategies, the staff is much more likely to successfully implement change. Schools can often change their schedules to create time for this by adding about 10 minutes every day and then releasing students earlier (or having them arrive later) once a week.

Help of Older Students

Older students can also provide support for integrating technology once teachers have a vision and a plan. Older children can act as mentors, so that younger children can execute their ideas without getting stuck on the difficulties of using the technology itself. Teachers often appreciate their help, too. In some schools, the technology coordinator recruits and trains interested older students to be part of a team of "Tech Wizards," who then help in the classrooms.

Involvement of Parents and Community

Parents and community members need to be involved in building the instructional vision that includes technology integration. If they are included from the beginning, there will be many ways that they can support the school. In most communities, there are at least some members who are very knowledgeable about technology and would be willing to help. For example, in one school a community volunteer held a weekly early morning support session to answer teachers' technical questions.

Use of Data for Continuous Improvement

Schools that develop authentic assessment strategies to complement more traditional student learning data have a better way to assess their progress in the area of student learning. Schools also need data about school processes (for example, what is actually being implemented) and perceptions to understand how well they are doing and what they need to change to improve.

A Plan for Equipment Maintenance

Maintaining the hardware and the network has to be thought out from the beginning. Some teachers will be able to help troubleshoot problems, but schools should not expect classroom teachers to be responsible for maintaining all the equipment. Costs of maintenance must be built into the budget, either at the school or district level.

Summary

Making schools more responsive to the ways children learn and develop is always a difficult journey. The change process becomes all the more complex when teachers and students are learning to use new technologies. Yet the experiences of schools that have taken this journey show that the benefits are well worth the effort.

When technology tools are used by students to create original work, they can provide support for exploring ideas and presenting them at a higher level than would otherwise be possible. Production tools such as word processors, digital cameras, and multimedia software provide the scaffolding for developing and communicating ideas. Communication tools such as e-mail and Web publishing give students real audiences and motivate them to improve the quality of their work. When technology tools are used for projects that are developmentally appropriate they enable children to have a high degree of control over their work as they construct knowledge.

References

Glickman, C.D. (1993). *Renewing America's schools: A guide for school-based action*. San Francisco: Jossey-Bass.

Means, B., K. Olson, and R. Singh. (1995, September). Beyond the classroom: Restructuring schools with technology. *Phi Delta Kappan, 77,* 69–72.

Papert, S.A. (1980). *Mindstorms: Children, computers, and powerful ideas*. New York: Basic Books.

Papert, S.A. (1993). *The children's machine: Rethinking school in the age of the computer*. New York: Basic Books.

10

Child Development Theory and Educational Practice

Although fairly stable and predictable sequences of human development appear to exist, a major premise of developmentally appropriate practice is that each child is unique and has an individual pattern and timing of growth.

Bredekamp and Copple, 1997

This chapter is included as a resource for those readers who would like a brief review of the child development theory that forms the basis for best practices in programs that serve children through the third grade. The idea of applying child development theory to instructional design is hardly new, but awareness among educators has grown significantly since 1987, when the National Association for the Education of Young Children (NAEYC) published its position on developmentally appropriate practices (Bredecamp, ed. 1987). Three years later the NAEYC and the National Association of Early Childhood Specialists in State Departments of Education (NAECS/SDE) jointly issued *Guidelines for Appropriate Curriculum Content and Assessment in Programs Serving Children Ages 3 through 8* (1990), which addresses the content of curriculum and assessment as well as pedagogy. In concert with other school reform documents, these two guidelines have influenced the nature of teaching and learning in primary education as well as in preschools.

Under the revised NAEYC guidelines (Bredecamp and Copple, eds. 1997), educators have a responsibility to design instructional programs based upon knowledge of:

♦ Child development, which allows schools to predict what kinds of activities will be challenging, achievable, and interesting to children in certain age ranges.

♦ The development, interests, and specific needs of the individual children served.

♦ The families and community that provide the social and cultural context necessary to make the children's experiences in school meaningful.

Although the second two factors must be determined at each site, the NAEYC notes 12 basic principles of child development that should inform instructional practices, as shown on page 166.

Summary of NAEYC's Basic Child Development Principles

1. Development in the social, emotional, physical, and cognitive domains are all related, and affect each other.

2. There are predictable patterns of development in all four domains. Curriculum planning aligned to these patterns allows students to make significant gains.

3. Children develop at different rates, and each child develops in the different domains at different rates. Additionally, children differ in terms of interest, culture, learning style, and personality. Rigid adherence to age-defined expectations is not an appropriate way of achieving high standards.

4. Early experiences have a cumulative effect on development. Some types of learning, such as language development, occur best at certain points in the developmental process. Verbal communication among young children is important and should be encouraged.

5. Cognitive development is predictable, becoming increasingly more complex and organized. Children's learning occurs first at the behavioral level, and only later can be represented symbolically. Early childhood programs should be rich in firsthand experiences and opportunities for children to represent experiences through retelling, dictating or writing, art, drama, and other means.

6. Development is influenced by the social and cultural context in which it occurs. This context influences child development on many levels.

7. Children construct knowledge through direct experience with the physical world and through social/cultural experiences. DAP draws upon the work of many theorists, who stress the importance of extensive opportunities for children to observe, record, form and test their own hypotheses, reflect, and reshape their understanding.

8. Both biological maturation and experience influence development and learning. While development follows a predictable path, teachers need to make sure that children have the experiences that encourage development.

9. Play is an important vehicle for development and growth. Children use their play for reflection, forming new mental structures. This is often most evident in dramatic play, but occurs in almost all forms of play. Play should be built into the early childhood curriculum.

10. Development occurs most when children are learning at their "growing edge" (Berk and Winsler, 1995). Continued motivation requires that activities be challenging and that children be successful most of the time. Adults and peers can provide scaffolding, the support children need when they work just beyond what they can do alone.

11. Children learn through many different modalities and intelligences; teachers should encourage children to demonstrate their knowledge through different modalities and intelligences. The role of the teacher is to build on children's strength, while supporting development in other areas.

12. Children develop best in an environment that is safe, caring, and provides for their emotional, social, and physical needs as well as academic needs.

The principles of the NAEYC have a long history of research and testing behind them. Any discussion of best practices in pre-kindergarten through third-grade should incorporate these principles, whether the discussion is about teaching reading or using technology. When schools erroneously assume that these principles apply only to preschools and kindergartens, they do a great disservice to their other young learners.

A Closer Look at Two Major Theories

Two researchers of the twentieth century, Jean Piaget and Lev Vygotsky, stand out as primary theorists of child development.

The Work of Jean Piaget

Much of the current understanding of how children learn and develop is based upon the work of the Swiss child psychologist Jean Piaget, who first developed the theory that children mature through identifiable stages of cognitive development. Piaget and the developmental stage theorists are set apart from other learning theory researchers because they believe that developmental stages exist that are qualitatively distinct from each other (Gruber and Voneche 1977).

Through extensive observations of children in problem-solving and social situations, Piaget identified four stages of development, as shown in Figure 10.1, which he believed apply to all children in all cultures.

To understand the impact of Piaget's work on early childhood education, the preoperational and concrete operational stages are particularly relevant.

The Preoperational Stage of Development

As children approach the preoperational stage (approximately ages two to seven), they begin to exhibit behaviors that indicate that they are forming internal representations of external actions. Speech becomes well developed during this period, but many other behaviors, such as pretend play, demonstrate symbolic thinking (Van Hoorn, Nourot, Scales, and Alward 1999). Yet the child's ability to reason is quite different from that of an older child.

Figure 10.1. Developmental Stages as Described by Piaget

Stage	Typical Characteristics
Sensorimotor	• Modifies physical reflexes to achieve a goal • Begins to represent objects and events with symbols, e.g., movement and words Approximate age: birth to 2 years
Preoperational	• Reasoning is one-dimensional • Thought tends to be highly egocentric Approximate age: 2 to 7 years
Concrete Operational	• Uses logic to solve concrete problems • Needs concrete experiences from which to develop and test hypotheses Approximate age: 7 to 11 years
Formal Operational	• Uses logic to solve both concrete and abstract problems • Is able to use inference Approximate age: 11 years and older

That children's thinking is highly egocentric is evident when one listens to preschool children converse. While they follow the conventions of conversations and take turns in speaking, the content is often more like separate monologues. When they are asked to categorize objects, they will often form categories such as "buttons I like," providing a glimpse into their egocentric view of the world.

Children in the preoperational stage of development have a very different view of causality than do older children. They tend to assume that two events that they experience together are linked, even if there is no real relationship between the two. Piaget referred to this as *phenomenalistic causality*. As a result, children sometimes develop what appears to adults to be irrational fears, but which may be quite rational from the child's understanding of causality.

A kindergarten student seemed to be constantly worried about spills. During a parent-teacher conference, her mother explained why. Her daughter had spilled juice several months earlier. As they began cleaning it up, the phone rang with a message that an older sibling had been hurt in an accident at school. The mother had been visibly shaken as she whisked her daughter away to pick up the older child. No amount of explaining seemed to resolve the child's worry that spilling juice can hurt people.

As told to the author

Similarly, adults are sometimes surprised by the child's difficulty in solving what appears to be a simple problem. Piaget's classic experiment is a case in point that indicates two aspects of young children's thinking. Children reported that a tall, thin glass had more water than a short, wide glass, even though they saw the same amount of water poured from two identical glasses into the different containers (Piaget and Szeminska 1952). Problem-solving at this stage of development tends to be one-dimensional; in this case, the children only considered the height of the water in the glass. Secondly, children at this stage have not yet mastered concepts of conservation, such as understanding that the amount of water is conserved even though the shape of the container changes.

A personal story from years as a kindergarten teacher illustrates this preoperational thinking:

Before Easter, I would usually hide chocolate eggs in the park behind our school and take the children out to hunt for them. They would bring the eggs to me and put them in a bag to share in the classroom. One year, the grass had just been cut, and the children found the eggs immediately. They were so disappointed when they could find no more that I reached into the bag and threw out a handful of the chocolate eggs that they had just collected. They squealed with delight, so I threw out another handful, and then another. "There are so many eggs!" they all agreed. Not a single child questioned this view.

Author's journal, 1980

Traditionally, elementary school teachers have asked children in the preoperational stage of development to *apply* concepts of causality and quantification to problems, rather than provide students with many opportunities to *develop* these concepts. From a developmental point of view, the preoperational child is better served by exploring a rich environment in which there are many opportunities both to observe and manipulate real objects and to describe and record ideas.

The Concrete Operational Stage of Development

As children move to the concrete operational period, on average between ages seven and eleven, they acquire the ability to "mentally manipulate their internal representation" (Siegler 1986). Their thinking becomes multidimensional, but is still based on mental representations of direct experiences and real objects. Changes in the child's mental processes as they move into this stage have significant implications for teaching and learning.

For one thing, children are now able to quantify objects in the world around them because they have developed the concept of a unit and can separate properties of objects from the objects. They not only can classify objects in much more subtle ways than before, but they can also understand subsets of categories, as evidenced by their interest in collecting and categorizing rocks, stamps, and other objects. Children in this stage are no longer confused when water from one glass is poured into another glass of a different shape.

Rules become very important to children in the concrete operational stage of development. Unlike younger children, who tend to make up rules as they go along, they play games with complicated rules and feel very strongly that rules should be applied consistently.

> Students in a second grade class have been corresponding with adult e-mail buddies. At the beginning of the year, the class set up rules about when they could use e-mail. The children could go to the computer any time except during circle time at the beginning of the day, during a group lesson in language arts or math, or when the teacher read a story to the whole class. After a long illness, one child returned to find several e-mails waiting. The teacher was surprised by the outcry that occurred when she suggested that just this once, a child could check e-mail during storytime.
>
> As told to the author

Because reasoning skills of children begin to resemble the reasoning skills of adults, adults may incorrectly assume that children's thinking at this stage is the same as that of adults. This is far from the case. Only in the formal operational stage, which Piaget identified as beginning at approximately age twelve, does the child become able to think highly abstractly, examining possibilities which are not based upon real experience, and systematically considering all possible solutions to a problem. While a child in the concrete operational stage might think of several possible ways to solve a difficult problem, a child in the formal operational stage will create a system for creating solutions so as not to omit any possibilities. (Researchers have since observed that the age at which people reach the formal operational stage varies greatly and that not everyone reaches this stage of development in all areas of thought.)

Piaget and Constructivism

Piaget has been accused by some critics of being rigid in his assignment of stages of development to specific ages, and of ignoring the impact of culture on development. Although Piaget observed clearly distinctive patterns in each developmental stage, he also acknowledged that the timing of these patterns varies and is influenced by environmental factors such as culture and previous experience. Although he did not focus on examining the impact of culture as did Vygotsky, his view of how children construct knowledge—to which he gave the term *constructivism*—gives credence to the importance of both culture and experience in his theories.

Piaget compares the way a child constructs his view of reality based on his own experience to the way an artist constructs a painting. No matter how lifelike the painting may appear to be, it is always "a unique combination of what the artist has taken from experience and what she has added to it from her own scheme of the world" (Elkind 1976).

According to Piaget, knowledge is organized and stored in the mind in patterns or structures called schemata. Schemata provide the framework through which learning and comprehension occur. Perception is an active process of construction through existing schema—the cumulative cognitive structures. An individual's schema strongly influences perception and in turn is influenced by perception.

For example, a young child looks at a globe and sees a brightly colored round ball. An adult looks at the same globe and sees a representation of the world. The child has learned by rote that the globe represents the world, but doesn't really understand. It will take many years of developing map knowledge, beginning with mapping the classroom, the school, the block, and so forth, as well as to time to mature and become a more abstract thinker, before the child can make the connections necessary to truly understand what globes represent.

Piaget describes two ways in which knowledge is developed—through *assimilation* and *accommodation*. The individual fits perceptions of the environment into existing schemata by means of assimilation. However, there are times when perceptions do not fit, resulting in a state of *disequilibrium* that forces the individual to rethink what is known. The process of accommodation is one of adjusting schemata to fit new knowledge, thus reestablishing equilibrium. It is through accommodation that the larger breakthroughs in learning occur.

For example, many K–1 classrooms use water or sand tables to give children the concrete experiences that are necessary for development. Through play, reflection, discussions with their peers and the teacher, and documentation, children come to know that a tall narrow container does not necessarily hold more than a short wide container simply because the fill line is higher. Conflict between the sum of the child's experience and what was previously "known" forces accommodation to occur.

> *Research on developmental stages that focuses primarily on the interaction between environmental factors such as culture and prior experience is complementary, not contrary, to Piaget's work.*

Piaget's model of constructivism is an important component of his theory of development. Because he theorized that perception of the environment both shapes the individual's schema and is shaped by it, it would be unreasonable to interpret Piaget's stages of development as rigidly age-defined or unaffected by culture.

In fact, some researchers believe that the criticisms described above derive from misinterpretation and overlook the constructivist, developmental nature of Piaget's work (Lourenco and Machado 1996). In keeping with this interpretation, research on developmental stages that focuses primarily on the interaction between environmental factors such as culture and prior experience is complementary, not contrary, to Piaget's work.

Applying Piaget's Work to the Classroom

Long before the term *developmentally appropriate practices* existed, Elkind (1976) presented a Piagetian perspective on the use of child development theory in the classroom. His points contain many elements of DAP, despite differences in vocabulary. The points are shown on page 174.

The Work of Lev Vygotsky

Lev Vygotsky, a Russian researcher who was a contemporary of Piaget, stressed the interaction between the child and the social-cultural environment as a central aspect of development. Although Vygotsky was familiar with Piaget's work, his own work was not readily available in English through the period of the Cold War.

Like Piaget, Vygotsky observed distinct stages of development. However, his work emphasizes three important concepts (Cunningham 1996):

- Learning can lead children in their development from one stage to the next.

- Language plays a central role in cognitive development.

- Development takes place in a social and historical context.

Vygotsky's thinking has had a major impact on recent educational practices, although many teachers may not be directly familiar with his work.

Learning Leads Development

Vygotsky identified three existing theories that explain the relationship between development and learning (Vygotsky 1978):

- Development and learning are independent of each other.

- Learning and development are the same. The child is simply an inexperienced learner who develops as he or she gains skills.

- Learning and development are distinct from each other but influence each other. Learning through experience affects development, and development affects learning.

To these he added his own theory, that learning leads development when the child is assisted in the learning experience at a level just beyond the child's actual developmental level—what he or she could do alone—in what Vygotsky called *the zone of proximal development*.

Applying Piaget to Instruction (Elkind 1976)

1. *Qualitative knowledge precedes quantitative knowledge.* Children need to spend a great deal of time classifying and serializing objects by characteristic before they can quantify them.

2. *Horizontal elaboration precedes vertical integration.* Children need to apply new concepts in a wide variety of situations. It is incorrect to push children to move on to the next more complex concept (vertical integration) and not allow them time to fully consolidate their knowledge (horizontal elaboration).

3. *The absolute precedes the relative.* Young children begin understanding concepts from an egocentric point of view. This is appropriate to their stage of development, and parents and teachers should not view it as wrong.

4. *Proximal experience precedes distal experience.* Through the concrete operational stage, children learn best from instruction that is connected to direct experience.

5. *Fluency precedes accuracy.* Especially in the area of literacy development, children need to work at creating meaning without being saddled with an adult insistence on accuracy. Adult attention to correcting the child's errors tends to inhibit fluency.

6. *Quality of practice is more important than quantity.* Motivation and attention are the most important variables in the beginning that requires practice (rote learning).

7. *Present the skill at the child's level of competence.* When adults assume understanding that is beyond the developmental level of the child, the child's confidence and willingness to tackle problems suffers.

8. *Social interaction and learning are related.* Piaget understood that the emotional attachments to teachers, peers, and older students that occur in the classroom is a powerful motivator in learning.

9. *Teachers can learn how to nurture the child's development by becoming careful observers.* Children's casual comments often reveal their level of cognitive functioning and provide clues about the support they need for further growth.

10. *Assessment should be based on documentation and observation.* Collecting actual student work over time provides valuable information for assessment.

11. *Standardized achievement tests are not appropriate.* Piaget referred to these tests as "a veritable plague on education at all levels" (1970, pp. 73–74), and felt that standardized tests become an end in themselves, encouraging rote learning that is unrelated to a person's ability to use knowledge.

12. *Instruction at the primary level should be rich in opportunities for children to manipulate objects, record observations, and enjoy children's literature.* Direct experiences facilitate operative (constructivist) rather than figurative (rote) learning.

13. *Children benefit from vertical (multiage) age grouping.* Piaget recognized interaction between children as important to cognitive development.

14. *Operative learning is neither totally child-directed nor totally teacher-directed.* The teacher's role is to guide the child's learning by providing rich experiences and interacting with the child in a flexible way.

The Zone of Proximal Development

Vygotsky measured the ability of children to solve problems alone, versus their ability to solve problems with assistance of a teacher or a more capable peer. Vygotsky believed that learning is best facilitated through collaboration with others in the range between the child's independent ability and what could be achieved with assistance—the zone of proximal development. He argued that instruction should be focused in this zone. The fallacy in the other theories, claimed Vygotsky, is that "even the profoundest thinkers never entertained the notion that what children can do with the assistance of others might be in some sense even more indicative of their mental development than what they can do alone" (Vygotsky 1978, p. 85).

> *Learning leads development when the child is assisted in the learning experience at a level just beyond the child's actual developmental level— what he or she could do alone— in the zone of proximal development.*

Within the zone of proximal development, access to adult or peer modeling and social communication makes it possible for children to work with concepts that are just beyond their independent ability. This modeling and external speech (conversation) later become internalized as the child develops concepts through interaction with others.

> A sixth grade student helped a second grade student create a multimedia presentation for the school science fair. The younger child had a difficult time choosing from the many pictures she had taken. The older child said, "Pick a picture that shows how you started your observation for the beginning screen." As the younger child looked through the pictures, she keeps repeating, "The beginning picture."
>
> As told to the author

Within this view, social interaction between the teacher or more capable peers and the learner can result in development that might not otherwise occur, or would not occur at that time (Bonk and King 1995).

Language Plays a Central Role in Learning

Language plays a central role in social interaction and communication, from which most learning first stems. This is not to suggest that the child learns by listening passively, but rather that the child constructs knowledge by collaborating with others in culturally meaningful activities (Berk and Winsler 1995). Learning first occurs through this social speech, which the child then internalizes.

> *The child constructs knowledge by collaborating with others in culturally meaningful activities.*

Vygotsky's examination of the *private language* of children—verbalizations that occur aloud as they solve problems—is helpful in understanding the relationship between learning and development. Not long after Piaget had characterized young children's monologues as *egocentric speech* that disappears as they mature, Vygotsky (1978) observed that children tend to talk to themselves more when they have a difficult problem to solve. Through these observations, he hypothesized that egocentric speech is "the transitional form between external and internal speech. Functionally, egocentric speech is the basis for inner speech" (Vygotsky 1978, p. 27). In later development, internal speech is a tool for planning and generally precedes action, while in young children, speech is used in social interaction to label actions after the fact.

From a Vygotskian point of view, the ability to use language internally to clarify thought is a milestone of human development. The use of internal language is also connected to memory; that is, it is an organizer by which humans extend natural memory. In younger children, thinking and recall are nearly the same; the child describes the world in terms of his or her own memories. "For the young child, to think means to recall, but for the adolescent, to recall means to think," wrote Vygotsky (1978, p. 51). At this point, the organization of thought changes from organization around memory or events to logical structures.

According to Vygotsky:

♦ All language develops from social interaction.

♦ Thought is the internalization of language.

♦ Memory is organized and extended by internal language.

♦ Therefore, thought and memory are to a great extent a product of social interaction.

Development Takes Place in a Social and Historical Context

Because Vygotsky focused his attention on the social aspect of learning through language, his work points out the influence of culture and history on the child's cognitive development. If language and symbols are cultural, and if learning that is based on language leads development, then language and symbols must have a major impact on development, according to the Vygotskian view. For example, cultures use language differently to express concepts of time, which become internalized. Similarly, some cultures develop unique symbolic language for abstract concepts that are not likely to develop in the individual without that language to express it (for example, Eskimo concepts of many distinct forms of snow).

> *Vygotsky's work points out the influence of culture and history on the child's cognitive development .*

Applying Vygotsky's Work to the Classroom

The argument of some computer educators in favor of teaching programming to young children is essentially a Vygotskian argument based on the connection between language and thought in our current historical context.

The argument goes as follows:

> Programming is a language that did not exist until recently. When we teach children this language, they are not merely able to think about ideas they have not thought about before, they are actually able to think differently. Programming has the ability to change not just what children think, but *the way* in which children think.

Seymour Papert, the inventor of LOGO and a student of Piaget's, makes this argument in his landmark book *Mindstorms: Children, Computers, and Powerful Ideas* (1980). He believes that when children control the computer by programming, their thought processes actually change, allowing them to think in ways that many adults cannot. While there is little conclusive evidence one way or the other for this theory, there is no doubt that language has an impact on conceptual development.

Cooperative Learning

Cooperative learning as an instructional strategy is an outgrowth of Vygotsky's theory. Cooperative group work can be most successful in terms of cognitive growth when teachers structure work in cooperative groups to fall within the zone of proximal development (Slavin 1987). Case studies of collaborative writing with a partner suggests that students internalize the scaffolding of more capable peers (Daiute and Dalton 1992). Students may also internalize the cognitive supports provided by computer tools (Solomon 1986).

Summary

Child development theory should provide the backdrop for examining classroom practices, especially in the primary grades (K–3). Despite variations in child development theories, certain principles can be found in the works of all major researchers, and form the bases of developmentally appropriate practices. Activities that involve technology are no different from other activities in that their design should take into consideration:

- Children's real experiences
- Children's varying stages of development, interests, and needs
- Children's varying cultures and languages

Teachers, technology coordinators, and curriculum planners have a responsibility to work together with parents to ensure that technology is used in ways that are consistent with child development theory, and that support both cognitive and social development of children.

References

Berk, L.E. and A. Winsler. (1995). *Scaffolding children's learning: Vygotsky and early childhood education.* Washington, D.C.: National Association for the Education of Young Children.

Bonk, C. and K. King (1995). Computer conferencing and collaborative writing tools: Starting a dialogue about student dialogue. In *CSCL '95: Proceedings of the first international conference on computer support for collaborative learning,* edited by J.L. Schnase and E.L. Cunnius. Mahwah, N.J.: Lawrence Erlbaum Associates.

Bredekamp, S., ed. (1987). *Developmentally appropriate practice in early childhood programs serving children from birth through age 8.* Washington, D.C.: National Association for the Education of Young Children.

Bredekamp, S. and C. Copple, ed. (1997). *Developmentally appropriate practice in early childhood programs.* Rev. ed. Washington, D.C.: National Association for the Education of Young Children.

Cunningham, D. (1996). Indiana University, Bloomington. http://education.indiana.edu/~cep/courses/p540/p540_1.html

Daiute, C. and B. Dalton. (1992). *Collaboration between children learning to write: Can novices be masters?* Berkeley, Calif.: National Center for the Study of Writing and Literacy.

Elkind, D. (1976). *Child development and education: A Piagetian perspective.* New York: Oxford University Press.

Gruber, H.E. and J.J. Voneche. (1977). *The essential Piaget.* New York: Basic Books.

Lourenco, O. and A. Machado. (1996). In defense of Piaget's theory: A reply to 10 common criticisms. *Psychological Review* 103 (1): 143–164.

National Association for the Education of Young Children and National Association of Early Childhood Specialists in State Departments of Education. (1990). *Guidelines for appropriate curriculum content and assessment in programs serving children ages 3 through 8.* Washington D.C.: National Association for the Education of Young Children.

Papert, S.A. (1980). *Mindstorms: Children, computers, and powerful ideas.* New York: Basic Books

Piaget, Jean (1970). *Science of education and the psychology of the child.* New York: Orion Press.

Piaget, J. and A. Szeminska. (1952). *The child's conception of number.* New York: Humanities Press.

Siegler, R. S. (1986). *Children's thinking.* Englewood Cliffs, N.J.: Prentice Hall.

Slavin, R.E. (1987). Developmental and motivational perspectives on cooperative learning: A reconciliation. *Child Development,* 58 (5), 1161–1167.

Solomon, C. (1986). *Computer environments for children: A reflection on theories of learning and education.* Cambridge, Mass.: MIT Press.

Vygotsky, L.S. (1978). In M. Cole, V. John-Steiner, S. Scribner, and E. Souberman, eds. *Mind in society: The development of higher psychological processes.* Cambridge, Mass.: Harvard University Press.

Van Hoorn, J., P.M. Nourot, B. Scales, and K.R. Alward. (1999). *Play at the center of the curriculum.* 2nd ed. New York: Merrill.

Appendices

Interview Participants

Millie Almy, Ph.D., is Professor Emerita of the Graduate School of Education at the University of California at Berkeley. Dr. Almy was among the first researchers to write about the application of Piaget's theories in educational settings. She was also an early advocate of using an interdisciplinary approach to serve children's needs in schools that brings together educators, psychologists, social workers, and health care professionals.

Jane Baldi is the school reform coordinator at Paden School (K–8), Alameda, California. Ms. Baldi has had a major role in creating a developmental program that connects classroom practices to child development theory, aligning school resources around that focus, and developing tools to support and to sustain developmental practices schoolwide.

Burke Cochran is a lecturer in the School of Education and a Faculty Developer in the Center for Teaching and Professional Development, Sonoma State University, Rohnert Park, California. Mr. Cochran was an elementary school teacher for 24 years with a strong interest in using technology to improve student learning. He was Teacher of the Year for Sonoma County in 1994 and has received numerous other awards for innovation in teaching.

Joyce Hakansson is a software designer, developer, and educator and the founder of Theatrix Interactive Software Company. Some of the award-winning software she has brought to the public include *Millie's Math House, Bailey's Book House, Hollywood,* and the *Juilliard Music Adventure*. Ms. Hakansson is also an experienced teacher and curriculum designer.

Cathaleen Hampton is a third grade teacher and the technology coordinator at Alvarado Elementary School, New Haven Unified School District, Union City, California. Ms. Hampton is a mentor teacher in technology. She has coordinated two technology staff development grants at the school and district level and is the program specialist for the Beginning Teacher Support and Assessment (BTSA) program for New Haven elementary schools. In 1998, she was honored as Teacher of the Year in her school district.

Linda Koistinen is the media center specialist at Haight Elementary School in Alameda, California. Ms. Koistinen has been involved in developing projects that use technology to bring together several areas of the curriculum. She has presented at conferences, developed teacher workshops for her district and other organizations about integrating technology, and written instructional units for the KQED public television Web site.

Patricia Nourot, Ph.D., is a professor in the School of Education, Sonoma State University, Rhonert Park, California. Dr. Nourot teaches classes in child development, educational theory, and early childhood curriculum. The focus of her writing has been in the area of children's play, including children's use of technology in play and how it relates to learning.

Barbara Scales, Ed.D., was head teacher and administrator of the Harold E. Jones Child Study Center, University of California at Berkeley, for over twenty years and is currently piloting new mathematics curriculum at the center and mentoring field test teachers as part of a federally funded math readiness project. Dr. Scales has conducted research on children's learning environments and on gender awareness in the school setting, and has written a number of books and articles on these and other topics.

Judith Van Hoorn, Ph.D., is a professor in the Benerd School of Education, University of the Pacific, Stockton, California. Dr. Van Hoorn teaches courses in child development and educational psychology. For the past two decades, she has focused her research and writing on the impact of culture on children's learning, play, and development, and on science education for young children.

Selected List of World Wide Web Resources

Pacific Bell Education First Elementary School Demonstration Sites

Bryant Elementary School
http://nisus.sfusd.k12.ca.us/schwww/sch456/index.html

Juarez-Lincoln Accelerated School
http://www.cvesd.k12.ca.us/jl

Mendocino Unified School District
http://www.mcn.org/ed/

Sites Related to Education First

Education for the Future Initiative
http://eff.csuchico.edu

Pacific Bell Knowledge Network
http://www.kn.pacbell.com/

Pacific Bell Fellows/San Diego State University
http://www.kn.pacbell.com/wired/

General Educational References and Links

Educational Resources Information Center (ERIC)
http://ericir.syr.edu/Eric

Instructional Technologies Connections, University of Colorado at Denver
http://www.cudenver.edu/~mryder/itcon.html

Vose Elementary School, Beaverton School District
http://www.beavton.k12.or.us/vose/index.html

Sources of Technology-infused Projects and Project Information

Blue Web'n, Pacific Bell Knowledge Network
http://www.kn.pacbell.com/wired/bluewebn/index.html

Cyberguides, Schools of California Online Resources for Education (SCORE)
http://www.sdcoe.k12.ca.us/score/cyberguide.html

Global Schoolhouse
http://www.gsh.org

Teams Distance Learning, Los Angeles County Office of Education
http://teams.lacoe.edu/

Specific Projects

Birds of a Feather, Jessica Morton, Mendocino Unified School District
http://www.mcn.org/ed/cur/liv/ind/birds/

Meet the Author, S. Quinn, R. Feder, L. Hutchison, T. Modelo, and K. Shoopack, Juarez-Lincoln Accelerated School
http://www.cvesd.k12.ca.us/jl

Monster Project, Brian Maguire, Winstar for Education
http://www.win4edu.com/minds-eye/monster/

Pumpkin Patch, Susan Silverman
http://www.webcom.com/suealice/pumpkins/welcome.html

Listservs and Newsgroups

Dejanews
http://www.dejanews.com/

Liszt
http://www.liszt.com/

Professional Organizations

National Educational Computing Association
http://www.neccsite.org/html/neca_cooperating_societies.html

Computer Problems

The California Technology Assistance Project (CTAP) Techcenter Help Desk
http://www.rims.k12.ca.us/ctap/help/macintosh/

Software Manuals

Peachpit Press
http://www.peachpit.com

Glossary

Accommodation. From Piaget. Adjustments in mental models as a result of conflicts between new experiences and what was previously known.

Address book. A personal list of e-mail addresses that is accessed with e-mail software.

Bandwidth. A measure of the quantity of information that can be transmitted per unit of time. Higher bandwidth lines carry more data and transmit the data faster.

Bulletin board. Virtual space on the Internet where messages and other information are shared.

CAD (Computer-Aided Design). Computer programs that are used to create engineering and architectural drawings, including perspective.

Chat room. Communication through the Internet that allows many users to be engaged simultaneously in a conversation.

Clip art. Simple, ready-made drawings provided in some computer programs that can be imported into other work.

Computer-based instruction; computer-based learning. Interactive computer programs that deliver instruction that is tailored by the user's responses.

Concrete operational stage. From Piaget. A stage of child development in which children are able to apply logical thought processes to problems they observe from direct experience.

Cooperative learning. A formal process in which students work together in groups, with each member of the group having specific responsibilities. Cooperative learning is related to Vygotsky's theories of child development.

Core literature. Reading that a school district requires of all students.

CU-See Me. Software that supports low-speed videoconferencing through the Internet.

Developmentally appropriate practices. Instructional practices based on principles of child development, and knowledge of the individual children and the cultural context from which they come.

Disequilibrium. From Piaget. A state of conflict in the individual's process of developing mental models (schemata) where two or more concepts conflict with each other, forcing the reconstruction of knowledge.

Egocentric speech. From Piaget. The habit of young children to speak aloud as they work and play.

Educational game software. A broad range of children's software that is meant to be both educational and entertaining. Many are interactive, adjusting the difficulty of the game to the user's responses.

E-mail Buddy. An adult or older student that mentors and supports a young child's writing through e-mail correspondence.

External speech. From Vygotsky. A young child's utterances, not necessarily aimed at communicating with others, that helps the child internalize concepts.

Formal operational stage. From Piaget. The final stage of development described by Piaget in which the child is able to apply abstract reasoning processes, including inference.

Frame Relay. A high speed telephone communications technology that provides bandwidth on demand.

Freeware. Software that is available without charge. Several sites on the Web offer freeware and shareware.

GIF. Graphic Interchange format. A common format for digital graphic images. GIF is currently the most universally accepted graphics file format on the World Wide Web.

Graphic images. Technically speaking, any images other than word-processed text, including some lettering. The term is used in this book to refer primarily to digital photos and artwork.

Growing edge. An expression to describe a child's work that is just beyond what the child could do unassisted. Based on Vygotsky's concept of the zone of proximal development. The term "learning edge" is sometimes used for the same concept.

Hotlist. On the Web, a list of Web sites that uses hypertext to allow the viewer to navigate from one site to another by clicking on the list.

HTML. Hypertext Markup Language. A simple programming language used for constructing Web pages.

Hypertext. Words that are used for navigation between parts of a multimedia presentation or Web site. Hypertext allows users to move from one part of the document to another part, or to other documents, in a nonlinear manner. Also see navigational buttons.

Interface, user interface. The aspect of a computer or computer program with which the user interacts, such as menus or toolbars. Most modern software utilizes a Graphical User Interface (GUI).

Inner speech. From Vygotsky. Thought that is verbalized internally.

Internet service provider (ISP). An organization that provides access to the Internet, either commercially or to members of its community.

ISDN. A higher speed, higher bandwidth telephone service than standard service that accommodates videoconferencing and Internet connection.

JPEG (JPG). A common format for saving graphic files, especially photographic images, often used on the Web. JPEG files can be compressed. JPEG gets its name from its developers, the Joint Photographic Experts Group.

Key Pal. A commonly used term for penpals that correspond by e-mail.

Listserv, Listserver. A form of communication by e-mail to a group of people who have a common interest. To post or receive communications, people must subscribe to the listserv. Listservs are generally free services.

Manipulatives. Concrete objects used by children to help them form concepts and solve problems, especially math and science concepts.

Memory hog. Slang for a computer program that takes up large amounts of memory to run; also used to refer to large files that take up large amounts of disk space.

Multimedia. A form of communication that is usually nonlinear and can include text, graphics, sound, video, and animation.

Navigational button. Used in multimedia presentations and Web pages, buttons allow the user to move from one part of the presentation to another in a nonlinear format. Also see Hypertext.

Operative learning. Learning that occurs when knowledge is constructed from experience.

PICT. A common Macintosh format for saving graphic files.

Preoperational stage. From Piaget. The stage of development before a child is able to apply logic to thought processes.

Quantification. The ability to conceptualize numerals as units of measure in which each unit is of equal value.

QuickTime Movie. A format for digital video files.

Reggio Emilia. A province in Italy that has developed a child-centered approach to early childhood education in which children document their observations and ideas in many different forms.

Router. A device used to forward data from one network to another, and through the Internet.

Scaffolding. Support that assists children in constructing their own knowledge in the zone of proximal development—the difference between what a child can achieve alone and what he or she can achieve with the help of an adult or more capable peer.

Scanner. A device that converts a paper image to a digital image that can be stored as a computer file. A scanner looks and functions like a small photocopier, but attaches directly to a computer where the image is stored.

Schema (singular), Schemata (plural). Mental models. Constructivists believe that learning is a process by which individuals build mental models that connect to previous learning.

Sensorimotor Stage. From Piaget. The earliest stage of development in which children develop control of sensory and motor functions.

Shareware. Software that is available for a minimal charge, usually on the honor system. Several sites on the Web offer freeware and shareware.

T1 line. A type of very high-speed telephone service that can support video-conferencing and Internet access for large computer networks.

Technology tools. Hardware or software that is used to create original work.

Telecommunications. A category of communications technology that uses phone lines as the underlying structure, such as e-mail or videoconferencing.

URL. Uniform Resource Locator. The address for an Internet site.

Video capture. A program used to convert video into digital computer files.

Videoconferencing. Two-way simultaneous communication of voice and video images.

Virtual field trip. A visit to a real place, using videoconferencing or the Internet to give the illusion of actually being there.

Virtual reality. An interactive multimedia environment that gives the illusion of three-dimensional reality, sometimes accompanied by sound.

Webmaster. The person who is responsible for maintaining a Web site.

Web page. One file in a collection of files that make up a Web site. On school Web sites, individual classes often have their own Web page.

Web Server. A powerful computer connected to the Internet at all times, on which Web sites reside and can be accessed by visitors.

Web, World Wide Web, WWW. The most commonly used organization of information on the Internet, which uses hypertext for moving from one document to another.

Web-authoring program. Multimedia software programs used to create Web pages.

Web site. A specific location on the Internet, housed on a Web server and accessible through an URL. A Web site may consist of many Web pages that are linked together.

Zone of proximal development. The difference between what a child can achieve alone and what he or she can achieve with the help of an adult or more capable peer.